AppCraft: The Ultimate Guide to Building Apps

Overview

"AppCraft: The Ultimate Guide to Building Apps" is a comprehensive book that will teach you everything you need to know about app building. Whether you are a beginner or an experienced developer, this book will guide you through the entire app development process. From understanding the fundamentals of app design to publishing and marketing your app, this book covers it all. With step-by-step instructions and practical examples, you will learn how to use the AppCraft software to create stunning and functional apps. Get ready to unleash your creativity and build amazing apps with AppCraft!

In the first part of the book, you will be introduced to the world of app building. You will learn about the app development process, how to choose the right app building software, and how to set up your development environment. Additionally, you will explore app design principles to create visually appealing and user-friendly apps.

Once you have a solid foundation, the book will guide you through the features and functionalities of AppCraft. You will learn how to install the software, create your first app, and navigate the AppCraft interface. Furthermore, you will gain a deep understanding of AppCraft components, allowing you to build complex and interactive apps.

Designing your app is a crucial step in the development process, and this book dedicates an entire chapter to it. You will learn how to plan your app's user interface, create app layouts and screens, and add colors, fonts, and images. Additionally, you will discover how to implement app navigation, enhance user experience with animations, and test and refine your app design. With the knowledge gained from this chapter, you will be able to create visually stunning and intuitive apps that users will love.

Working with data is an essential aspect of app development, and this book provides a comprehensive guide on how to handle it. You will learn about data models, creating and managing data sources, and fetching and displaying data in your app. Additionally, you will explore how to implement data validation and security measures to protect your app and user data. With the skills acquired in this chapter, you will be able to create apps that effectively handle and utilize data.

Adding functionality to your app is what makes it truly useful and engaging. In this chapter, you will learn how to work with AppCraft actions, implement user input and interactivity, and integrate APIs and services into your app. Furthermore, you will discover how to implement app notifications to keep users informed and engaged. By the end of this chapter, you will have the knowledge and skills to create powerful and feature-rich apps.

Publishing your app is the final step in the app development process, and this book provides a comprehensive guide on how to do it successfully. You will learn how to prepare your app for publishing, generate app builds for different platforms, and test and debug your app to ensure its quality. Additionally, you will discover how to submit your app to app stores and navigate the app store submission process. With the insights gained from this chapter, you will be able to confidently publish your app and make it available to users worldwide.

Marketing and monetization are crucial aspects of app development, and this book dedicates an entire chapter to them. You will learn how to create an app marketing strategy, optimize your app store listing to increase visibility, and implement in-app purchases and ads to monetize your app. Additionally, you will explore how to track and analyze app performance to make data-driven decisions. By the end of this chapter, you will have the knowledge and tools to effectively market and monetize your app.

In the advanced techniques chapter, you will learn how to take your app building skills to the next level. You will discover how to work with custom code to add unique functionalities to your app, implement advanced app features, optimize app performance for better user experience, and implement app localization to reach a global audience. With the advanced techniques covered in this chapter, you will be able to create highly customized and optimized apps.

Troubleshooting and debugging are inevitable parts of app development, and this book provides a comprehensive guide on how to handle them. You will learn about common AppCraft errors and their solutions, debugging techniques and tools, testing and fixing app performance issues, and handling user feedback and bug reports. With the troubleshooting and debugging skills acquired in this chapter, you will be able to effectively identify and resolve issues in your app.

To ensure that your app is of the highest quality, this book covers app building best practices in a dedicated chapter. You will learn how to write clean and maintainable code, implement app security measures to protect user data, optimize app user experience for better engagement, and stay up-to-date with AppCraft updates and industry trends. By following these best practices, you will be able to create apps that are reliable, secure, and user-friendly.

Case studies provide valuable insights and learning opportunities, and this book includes a chapter dedicated to them. You will explore successful AppCraft app examples to understand what makes an app successful, analyze app success stories to learn from real-world examples, and learn from app failures to avoid common pitfalls. Additionally, you will dive into a detailed case study that takes you through the entire app building process, from idea to launch. By studying these case studies, you will gain valuable knowledge and inspiration for your own app building journey.

In the final chapter of the book, you will find a recap of the AppCraft app building process, highlighting the key concepts and steps covered throughout the book. Additionally, you will discover the next steps in your app building journey, including resources for further learning and expanding your skills. The book concludes with final thoughts and a thank you, leaving you inspired and ready to embark on your app building journey.

1. Introduction to App Building

Understanding the App Development Process

App development is an exciting and rapidly growing field that allows individuals and businesses to create innovative and functional applications for various platforms such as smartphones, tablets, and computers. Whether you have a brilliant app idea or want to enhance your programming skills, understanding the app development process is crucial to successfully bring your ideas to life.

In this section, we will explore the fundamental concepts and steps involved in the app development process. We will discuss the key stages, from conceptualization to deployment, and provide you with a comprehensive understanding of what it takes to build a successful app.

Defining Your App Idea

The first step in the app development process is to define your app idea. This involves identifying the problem your app will solve, determining your target audience, and outlining the core features and functionalities of your app. It is essential to conduct thorough market research to ensure that your app idea is unique and has the potential to succeed in the competitive app market.

Planning and Wireframing

Once you have a clear app idea, the next step is to plan and create a wireframe for your app. A wireframe is a visual representation of your app's layout and functionality. It helps you map out the user interface (UI) and user experience (UX) design, ensuring that your app is intuitive and easy to navigate.

During the planning and wireframing stage, you should consider the flow of your app, the placement of buttons and menus, and the overall design aesthetics. This stage allows you to make necessary adjustments and improvements before moving forward with the development process.

Choosing the Right Development Approach

When it comes to app development, there are various approaches you can take, depending on your requirements and resources. The two primary development approaches are native app development and cross-platform app development.

Native app development involves building separate apps for each platform, such as iOS and Android, using platform-specific programming languages and tools. This approach offers the advantage of utilizing the full capabilities of each platform but requires more time and resources.

On the other hand, cross-platform app development allows you to build a single app that can run on multiple platforms. This approach uses frameworks like React Native or Flutter, which enable developers to write code once and deploy it across different platforms. Cross-platform development offers faster development cycles and cost savings but may have limitations in accessing certain platform-specific features.

Development and Testing

Once you have defined your app idea, planned the UI/UX, and chosen the development approach, it's time to start coding. During the development phase, you will write the code that brings your app to life. This involves implementing the app's features, integrating APIs and services, and handling user input and data.

It is crucial to follow best practices and coding standards during the development process to ensure the code's quality and maintainability. Regular testing is also essential to identify and fix any bugs or issues that may arise. Testing can be done manually or through automated testing frameworks to ensure that your app functions as intended on different devices and operating systems.

Deployment and Maintenance

Once your app is developed and thoroughly tested, it's time to deploy it to the app stores or distribute it through other channels. This involves creating developer accounts, preparing the necessary app assets, and adhering to the guidelines and requirements of each app store.

After your app is live, it's important to monitor its performance, gather user feedback, and release updates to improve its functionality and address any issues. Regular maintenance and updates are crucial to keep your app relevant and competitive in the ever-evolving app market.

Continuous Learning and Improvement

The app development process is not a one-time event but an ongoing journey of continuous learning and improvement. As technology advances and user expectations evolve, it is essential to stay updated with the latest trends, tools, and frameworks in the app development industry.

By continuously learning and improving your skills, you can enhance your app building capabilities and create more innovative and successful applications. Engaging with the app development community, attending conferences, and exploring online resources are great ways to stay informed and expand your knowledge.

In the next section, we will explore the different app building software available and help you choose the right one for your needs. Understanding the app development process is the foundation for building successful apps, and with the right tools and knowledge, you can turn your app ideas into reality.

Choosing the Right App Building Software

Choosing the right app building software is a crucial step in your journey to becoming an app developer. With so many options available in the market, it can be overwhelming to decide which software to use. In this section, we will explore the factors you should consider when choosing app building software and provide you with some popular options to consider.

Factors to Consider

Before diving into the various app building software options, it's important to understand the factors you should consider when making your decision. Here are some key factors to keep in mind:

Ease of Use

One of the most important factors to consider is the ease of use of the app building software. As a beginner, you want a software that has a user-friendly interface and intuitive features. Look for software that offers drag-and-drop functionality, pre-built templates, and a visual editor that allows you to see real-time changes as you build your app.

Platform Compatibility

Consider the platforms you want your app to be available on. Some app building software only supports specific platforms like iOS or Android, while others offer cross-platform capabilities. If you want your app to reach a wider audience, it's recommended to choose software that supports multiple platforms.

Customization Options

Every app is unique, and you may have specific design and functionality requirements. Look for software that offers a wide range of customization options, such as the ability to customize the user interface, add custom code, and integrate with third-party services. The more flexibility the software provides, the better you can tailor your app to meet your specific needs.

Cost

Consider your budget when choosing app building software. Some software options are free, while others require a subscription or one-time payment. Take into account any additional costs, such as hosting fees or fees for publishing your app to app stores. It's important to find a balance between cost and the features and capabilities offered by the software.

Support and Documentation

When you encounter issues or have questions during the app building process, it's important to have access to reliable support and documentation. Look for software that offers comprehensive documentation, tutorials, and a responsive support team. This will help you overcome any obstacles you may face and ensure a smooth app development experience.

Popular App Building Software Options

Now that you understand the factors to consider, let's explore some popular app building software options:

AppCraft

AppCraft is a powerful and user-friendly app building software that is suitable for both beginners and experienced developers. It offers a drag-and-drop interface, pre-built templates, and a wide range of customization options. With AppCraft, you can build apps for iOS, Android, and the web, making it a versatile choice. It also provides comprehensive documentation and a supportive community to help you along your app building journey.

Appy Pie

Appy Pie is a popular no-code app building software that allows you to create apps without any coding knowledge. It offers a simple drag-and-drop interface and a wide range of pre-built templates and features. Appy Pie supports both iOS and Android platforms and provides options for e-commerce integration, push notifications, and more. It offers different pricing plans to suit various needs and budgets.

Flutter

Flutter is an open-source UI software development kit created by Google. It allows you to build beautiful and high-performance apps for iOS, Android, and the web using a single codebase. Flutter uses the Dart programming language and offers a rich set of pre-built widgets and tools. It is a popular choice for developers who want more control and flexibility in their app development process.

React Native

React Native is another popular open-source framework for building cross-platform apps. Developed by Facebook, it allows you to build native-like apps for iOS and Android using JavaScript and React. React Native offers a large community and a wide range of third-party libraries and plugins, making it a flexible choice for app development.

Making Your Decision

When choosing the right app building software, it's important to evaluate your specific needs and goals. Consider the factors discussed in this section and explore the options available in the market. Take advantage of free trials or demos to get hands-on experience with the software before making your final decision. Remember, the right app building software will empower you to bring your app ideas to life and make the app development process enjoyable and efficient.

Setting Up Your Development Environment

Setting up your development environment is an essential step in the app building process. It involves configuring your computer with the necessary tools and software to create, test, and deploy your apps. In this section, we will guide you through the process of setting up your development environment for app building.

Choosing the Right Operating System

Before you start setting up your development environment, it's important to choose the right operating system (OS) for app development. The most common choices are Windows, macOS, and Linux. Each OS has its own advantages and disadvantages, so consider your specific needs and preferences when making a decision.

Windows is a popular choice for app development due to its wide compatibility with various software and tools. It offers a user-friendly interface and extensive support for development environments. If you are already familiar with Windows, it may be the most convenient option for you.

macOS, on the other hand, is the preferred choice for many developers, especially those working on iOS apps. It provides a seamless integration with Apple's development tools and frameworks, making it easier to build and test iOS apps. If you are targeting the Apple ecosystem, macOS is highly recommended.

Linux is a powerful and flexible OS that is widely used by developers. It offers a high level of customization and control, making it a popular choice for advanced users. Linux is particularly suitable for web and server-side app development. If you prefer an open-source environment and have experience with Linux, it can be a great option.

Installing a Code Editor

A code editor is an essential tool for app development. It allows you to write, edit, and manage your app's source code. There are many code editors available, each with its own features and capabilities. Here are some popular choices:

- **Visual Studio Code**: Visual Studio Code (VS Code) is a lightweight and versatile code editor developed by Microsoft. It supports a wide range of programming languages and offers a rich set of features, including code completion, debugging, and version control integration. VS Code is highly extensible through its vast library of extensions, making it a popular choice among developers.

- **Sublime Text**: Sublime Text is a popular code editor known for its speed and simplicity. It provides a clean and intuitive interface and offers powerful features such as multiple cursors, split editing, and a command palette. Sublime Text is highly customizable and supports a wide range of programming languages.

- **Atom**: Atom is an open-source code editor developed by GitHub. It is built on web technologies and offers a modern and customizable interface. Atom provides a rich ecosystem of packages and themes, allowing you to tailor the editor to your needs. It also supports Git integration and has a built-in package manager.

Choose a code editor that suits your preferences and workflow. It's important to feel comfortable and productive while working with your chosen editor.

Installing a Software Development Kit (SDK)

A Software Development Kit (SDK) is a collection of tools and libraries that enable developers to build apps for a specific platform or framework. Depending on the platform you are targeting, you will need to install the corresponding SDK. Here are some commonly used SDKs:

- **Android SDK**: If you are developing Android apps, you will need to install the Android SDK. It provides the necessary tools, libraries, and APIs to build, test, and debug Android applications. The Android SDK includes the Android Studio IDE, which is the official integrated development environment for Android app development.

- **iOS SDK**: For iOS app development, you will need to install the iOS SDK, which is part of Apple's Xcode development environment. Xcode provides a comprehensive set of tools, including an IDE, simulator, and debugging tools, to develop, test, and deploy iOS apps. Xcode is only available on macOS.

- **React Native SDK**: If you are using React Native to build cross-platform apps, you will need to install the React Native SDK. It includes the necessary tools and libraries to develop, test, and deploy React Native apps on both Android and iOS platforms. The React Native SDK works with any code editor and does not require a specific IDE.

Make sure to follow the installation instructions provided by the SDK documentation to set up the necessary tools and dependencies.

Setting Up a Version Control System

Version control is crucial for managing your app's source code and collaborating with other developers. It allows you to track changes, revert to previous versions, and merge code changes seamlessly. One of the most popular version control systems is Git.

To set up Git, you will need to install it on your computer and configure it with your preferred code editor. Git provides a command-line interface, but there are also graphical user interfaces (GUIs) available, such as GitHub Desktop and Sourcetree, which provide a more user-friendly experience.

Once you have installed Git, create a new repository for your app's source code. This will serve as a central repository where you can push your code and collaborate with others. You can also use popular code hosting platforms like GitHub, GitLab, or Bitbucket to host your repositories and facilitate collaboration.

Installing Additional Tools and Libraries

Depending on the specific requirements of your app, you may need to install additional tools and libraries. For example, if you are building a web app, you may need to install a web server like Apache or Nginx. If you are working with databases, you may need to install a database management system like MySQL or MongoDB. It's important to research and identify the necessary tools and libraries for your app's development. Consult the documentation and resources available for the platform or framework you are using to ensure you have all the required dependencies installed. Setting up your development environment is a crucial step in the app building process. By choosing the right operating system, installing a code editor, setting up an SDK, configuring a version control system, and installing additional tools and libraries, you will have a solid foundation for developing your apps. In the next chapter, we will dive into AppCraft and explore how to get started with building your first app.

Exploring App Design Principles

Design is a crucial aspect of app development. It is what makes an app visually appealing, user-friendly, and intuitive. In this section, we will explore the fundamental principles of app design that will help you create engaging and successful apps.

User-Centered Design

User-centered design is a design approach that focuses on the needs and preferences of the end-users. It involves understanding the target audience, their goals, and their expectations from the app. By putting the user at the center of the design process, you can create an app that meets their needs and provides a positive user experience.

To implement user-centered design, you need to conduct user research and gather insights about your target audience. This can be done through surveys, interviews, and usability testing. By understanding the users' preferences, behaviors, and pain points, you can design an app that addresses their specific needs.

Consistency and Visual Hierarchy

Consistency is a key principle in app design. It ensures that the app's elements, such as buttons, icons, and typography, are visually consistent throughout the app. Consistency helps users navigate the app easily and understand its functionality. It also creates a sense of familiarity and builds trust with the users.

Visual hierarchy is another important aspect of app design. It refers to the arrangement and prioritization of elements based on their importance. By using visual cues such as size, color, and placement, you can guide the users' attention and help them understand the app's structure. For example, important actions or information can be highlighted using larger fonts or contrasting colors.

Simplicity and Minimalism

Simplicity and minimalism are design principles that emphasize the removal of unnecessary elements and clutter from the app interface. A simple and clean design not only enhances the app's visual appeal but also improves its usability. By reducing complexity, you can make the app easier to understand and navigate.

To achieve simplicity, focus on the core functionality of the app and eliminate any unnecessary features or distractions. Use white space effectively to create a sense of balance and clarity. Keep the user interface clean and uncluttered, with a minimal number of buttons and options. This will help users focus on the essential tasks and make their interaction with the app more efficient.

Intuitive Navigation

Navigation is a critical aspect of app design as it determines how users move through the app and access its various features. Intuitive navigation ensures that users can easily find what they are looking for and navigate between different screens or sections of the app.

To create intuitive navigation, consider the mental models and expectations of your target audience. Use familiar navigation patterns such as tab bars, side menus, or bottom navigation bars. Label navigation elements clearly and use visual cues such as icons or color to indicate the current location or active state. Provide feedback to users when they interact with navigation elements to confirm their actions.

Responsive Design

With the increasing use of mobile devices, it is essential to design apps that are responsive and adapt to different screen sizes and orientations. Responsive design ensures that the app's layout and content adjust dynamically to provide an optimal user experience on various devices.

To implement responsive design, use flexible layouts and grids that can adapt to different screen sizes. Prioritize content based on its importance and ensure that it remains accessible and readable on smaller screens. Test the app on different devices and screen resolutions to ensure that it looks and functions well across a range of devices.

Accessibility

Accessibility is an important consideration in app design to ensure that people with disabilities can use the app effectively. By designing for accessibility, you can make your app inclusive and reach a wider audience.

Consider the needs of users with visual impairments, hearing impairments, or motor disabilities. Provide alternative text for images, captions for videos, and transcripts for audio content. Use color contrast that is readable for users with visual impairments. Ensure that the app can be navigated using keyboard-only inputs for users with motor disabilities.

Branding and Visual Identity

Branding and visual identity play a significant role in app design. They help create a unique and memorable experience for users and establish a strong brand presence. Consistent branding across the app builds trust and recognition among users.

Consider the app's target audience and the brand's personality when designing the visual identity. Use appropriate colors, typography, and imagery that align with the brand's values and message. Create a cohesive visual language that is consistent with the brand's other marketing materials.

Usability Testing and Iteration

Usability testing is a crucial step in the app design process. It involves observing users as they interact with the app and gathering feedback to identify usability issues and areas for improvement. Usability testing helps validate design decisions and ensures that the app meets the users' needs.

Conduct usability testing with a diverse group of users to gather a range of perspectives. Observe how users navigate the app, complete tasks, and provide feedback on their experience. Use this feedback to iterate and refine the app's design, making it more user-friendly and intuitive.

By understanding and applying these app design principles, you can create visually appealing, user-friendly, and engaging apps that provide a positive user experience. Remember to keep the user at the center of the design process and iterate based on user feedback to continuously improve your app's design.

2.   Getting Started with AppCraft

Installing AppCraft

Before you can start building your own apps with AppCraft, you need to install the software on your computer. In this section, we will guide you through the installation process step by step.

System Requirements

Before you begin the installation, it's important to ensure that your computer meets the minimum system requirements for running AppCraft. These requirements may vary depending on the version of AppCraft you are installing, so it's always a good idea to check the official documentation for the most up-to-date information. However, here are the general system requirements:

- Operating System: AppCraft is compatible with Windows, macOS, and Linux operating systems. Make sure you have a supported version installed on your computer.
- Processor: A multi-core processor with a clock speed of at least 2 GHz is recommended for optimal performance.
- RAM: AppCraft requires a minimum of 4 GB of RAM, but it's recommended to have at least 8 GB for smoother operation.

- Storage: You will need a minimum of 2 GB of free disk space to install AppCraft and its associated files.
- Graphics Card: A dedicated graphics card with at least 1 GB of VRAM is recommended for better rendering performance.

Downloading AppCraft

To download AppCraft, you will need to visit the official website of the AppCraft platform. Once you are on the website, look for the "Download" or "Get Started" button, which will usually be prominently displayed on the homepage. Click on the button to initiate the download process.

AppCraft is available in different versions, including a free version with limited features and a paid version with additional functionality. Choose the version that best suits your needs and click on the corresponding download link.

Installing AppCraft

Once the download is complete, locate the installation file on your computer and double-click on it to start the installation process. The installation wizard will guide you through the necessary steps to install AppCraft on your system.

1. Language Selection: The installation wizard will prompt you to select the language for the installation process. Choose your preferred language from the available options and click "Next" to proceed.

2. License Agreement: Read the End User License Agreement (EULA) carefully and accept the terms and conditions to continue with the installation. Click "Next" to proceed.

3. Destination Folder: Choose the folder where you want to install AppCraft. The default location is usually in the "Program Files" directory on Windows or the "Applications" folder on macOS. You can also choose a different location by clicking on the "Browse" button. Once you have selected the destination folder, click "Next" to proceed.

4. Start Menu Folder: Choose whether you want to create a shortcut for AppCraft in the Start Menu (Windows) or Applications folder (macOS). You can also choose not to create a shortcut by unchecking the corresponding option. Click "Next" to proceed.

5. Additional Tasks: The installation wizard may offer additional tasks, such as creating a desktop shortcut or associating AppCraft with certain file types. Select the tasks you want to perform and click "Next" to proceed.

6. Ready to Install: Review the installation settings and click "Install" to begin the installation process. AppCraft will now be installed on your computer.

7. Installation Progress: The installation wizard will display the progress of the installation process. This may take a few minutes, depending on your computer's performance.

8. Installation Complete: Once the installation is complete, you will see a confirmation message. Click "Finish" to exit the installation wizard.

Launching AppCraft

After the installation is complete, you can launch AppCraft by locating the shortcut icon on your desktop (if you chose to create one) or by searching for "AppCraft" in the Start Menu (Windows) or Applications folder (macOS).

When you launch AppCraft for the first time, you may be prompted to sign in with your AppCraft account or create a new one. If you don't have an account yet, follow the on-screen instructions to create one.

Once you have signed in, you are ready to start building your first app with AppCraft. In the next section, we will guide you through the process of creating your first app using the AppCraft platform.

Congratulations on successfully installing AppCraft! You are now one step closer to becoming an app builder.

Creating Your First App

Now that you have installed AppCraft, it's time to dive into the exciting world of app building. In this section, we will guide you through the process of creating your very first app using AppCraft. Whether you are a beginner or have some experience in app development, this step-by-step guide will help you get started on your app building journey.

Defining Your App Idea

Before we jump into creating your first app, it's important to have a clear understanding of what you want to build. Take some time to brainstorm and define your app idea. Consider the purpose of your app, the target audience, and the problem it aims to solve. Having a well-defined app idea will guide you throughout the development process and help you stay focused on your goals.

Creating a New Project

To create your first app in AppCraft, you need to start by creating a new project. Follow these steps:

1. Launch AppCraft and click on the "New Project" button.
2. Give your project a name that reflects the purpose of your app.
3. Choose the platform you want to build your app for (e.g., iOS, Android, Web).
4. Select a template that closely matches the layout and design you have in mind for your app. This will provide you with a starting point to work with.

Understanding the AppCraft Workspace

Once you have created a new project, you will be greeted with the AppCraft workspace. Let's take a moment to familiarize ourselves with the different components of the workspace:

1. **Canvas**: This is the main area where you will design and build your app's user interface. You can drag and drop components onto the canvas to create screens and layouts.

2. **Component Library**: Located on the left side of the workspace, the component library contains a wide range of pre-built UI components that you can use in your app. These components include buttons, text fields, images, and more.
3. **Properties Panel**: The properties panel is located on the right side of the workspace. It allows you to customize the properties of the selected component, such as its size, color, and behavior.
4. **Toolbar**: The toolbar is located at the top of the workspace and provides quick access to various tools and features in AppCraft. Here, you can find options for saving your project, previewing your app, and exporting your app for testing or publishing.

Designing Your App's User Interface

Now that you are familiar with the AppCraft workspace, it's time to start designing your app's user interface. The user interface (UI) is the visual representation of your app and plays a crucial role in providing a seamless user experience. Follow these steps to design your app's UI:

1. Drag and drop components from the component library onto the canvas to create screens and layouts.
2. Use the properties panel to customize the appearance and behavior of each component. You can change the size, color, font, and other properties to match your app's design.
3. Arrange the components on the canvas to create a logical flow and hierarchy. Consider the user's journey through your app and ensure that the UI is intuitive and easy to navigate.
4. Use the alignment and spacing tools in AppCraft to ensure that your UI elements are properly aligned and evenly spaced.

Adding Functionality to Your App

Once you have designed your app's user interface, it's time to add functionality to your app. This is where you bring your app to life and make it interactive. Follow these steps to add functionality to your app:

1. Select a component on the canvas and go to the properties panel.
2. Look for the "Actions" section in the properties panel. Here, you can define the actions that will be triggered when the user interacts with the component.
3. Choose from a wide range of actions, such as navigating to another screen, displaying a message, or performing a calculation.
4. Configure the action parameters based on your app's requirements. For example, if you want to navigate to another screen, specify the target screen in the action parameters.

Previewing and Testing Your App

Once you have designed your app's UI and added functionality, it's important to preview and test your app to ensure everything is working as expected. AppCraft provides a built-in preview feature that allows you to see how your app will look and behave on different devices. Follow these steps to preview and test your app:

1. Click on the "Preview" button in the toolbar.
2. Choose the device or platform you want to preview your app on.
3. AppCraft will generate a preview of your app, allowing you to interact with it and test its functionality.
4. Use the preview feature to identify any issues or bugs in your app and make necessary adjustments.

Refining and Iterating Your App

App development is an iterative process, and it's common to refine and iterate on your app multiple times before it's ready for release. After previewing and testing your app, gather feedback from users or colleagues and make necessary refinements. Consider the following steps to refine and iterate your app:

1. Analyze user feedback and identify areas for improvement.
2. Make necessary changes to your app's UI, functionality, or performance based on the feedback received.

3. Test your app again to ensure that the changes have been implemented correctly and have improved the user experience.
4. Repeat this process until you are satisfied with the final version of your app.

Congratulations! You have successfully created your first app using AppCraft. In the next section, we will explore the different components of AppCraft in more detail, allowing you to unleash the full potential of the software.

Navigating the AppCraft Interface

Once you have installed AppCraft and created your first app, it's time to familiarize yourself with the AppCraft interface. Navigating the interface efficiently is essential for a smooth app building experience. In this section, we will explore the various components and features of the AppCraft interface, helping you become comfortable with its layout and functionality.

The Main Workspace

When you open AppCraft, you will be greeted with the main workspace, where you will spend most of your time building and designing your app. The main workspace consists of several key elements:

1. **Toolbar**: The toolbar is located at the top of the interface and provides quick access to various tools and functions. It typically includes buttons for actions such as saving, undo/redo, previewing the app, and publishing.

2. **Sidebar**: The sidebar is located on the left side of the interface and contains different panels that allow you to manage various aspects of your app. These panels may include the component library, data sources, app settings, and more. You can collapse or expand the sidebar as needed to maximize your workspace.

3. **Canvas**: The canvas is the central area of the interface where you design and build your app's user interface. It

represents the screen of your app and allows you to drag and drop components, arrange them, and customize their properties. The canvas provides a visual representation of how your app will look and behave.

4. **Inspector**: The inspector panel is typically located on the right side of the interface and provides detailed information and options for the selected component on the canvas. It allows you to modify properties such as size, position, styling, and behavior. The inspector panel adapts based on the selected component, providing relevant options and settings.

Component Library

The component library is an essential part of the AppCraft interface. It contains a wide range of pre-built components that you can use to build your app's user interface. These components include buttons, text fields, images, lists, menus, and more. To access the component library, you can click on the "Components" tab in the sidebar.

The component library is organized into categories, making it easy to find the component you need. You can browse through the categories or use the search bar to quickly locate a specific component. To add a component to your app, simply drag and drop it from the component library onto the canvas.

Once a component is added to the canvas, you can customize its properties using the inspector panel. You can change its size, position, styling, and behavior to match your app's design and functionality requirements. AppCraft provides a wide range of customization options, allowing you to create unique and visually appealing user interfaces.

AppCraft Editor

The AppCraft editor is where you can fine-tune the behavior and functionality of your app. It allows you to add actions, define event triggers, and implement logic to make your app interactive and responsive. To access the AppCraft editor, you can click on the "Actions" tab in the sidebar.

The AppCraft editor uses a visual programming approach, making it accessible to users without extensive coding knowledge. It provides a drag-and-drop interface for creating actions and defining their behavior. You can connect different components and events to create a flow of actions that respond to user interactions.

AppCraft offers a wide range of built-in actions that you can use to implement common app functionality. These actions include navigating between screens, displaying alerts, making API requests, and more. You can also create custom actions using JavaScript if you require more advanced functionality.

Previewing and Testing

AppCraft provides a built-in preview feature that allows you to see how your app will look and behave on different devices and screen sizes. You can access the preview mode by clicking on the "Preview" button in the toolbar. This feature is invaluable for testing your app's responsiveness and ensuring a consistent user experience across devices.

While previewing your app, you can interact with it as if it were running on a real device. This allows you to test the functionality and user interface in a realistic environment. If you encounter any issues or inconsistencies, you can make adjustments in the main workspace and instantly see the changes reflected in the preview.

In addition to the built-in preview feature, AppCraft also provides options for testing your app on actual devices. You can generate test builds for different platforms, such as iOS and Android, and install them on physical devices for thorough testing. This ensures that your app functions correctly and performs well on real-world devices.

Collaboration and Version Control

AppCraft offers collaboration and version control features that allow multiple team members to work on the same app simultaneously.

This is particularly useful for larger projects where different team members may be responsible for different aspects of the app.

The collaboration feature enables real-time collaboration, allowing team members to see each other's changes and work together seamlessly. It eliminates the need for manual merging of code or design changes and ensures that everyone is always working on the latest version of the app.

The version control feature allows you to track changes made to your app over time. It provides a history of modifications, allowing you to revert to previous versions if needed. This feature is especially helpful when experimenting with different design or functionality ideas, as it allows you to easily compare and revert changes. Navigating the AppCraft interface is a crucial step in becoming proficient in app building. Understanding the main workspace, component library, AppCraft editor, previewing and testing features, and collaboration tools will empower you to create stunning and functional apps. Take the time to explore each element of the interface and experiment with different components and actions to unleash your creativity and build amazing apps.

Understanding AppCraft Components

In order to effectively build apps using AppCraft, it is important to have a solid understanding of its components. AppCraft provides a wide range of components that you can use to create the user interface and functionality of your app. These components are like building blocks that you can assemble to create a fully functional app. In this section, we will explore the different types of components available in AppCraft and how you can use them to build your app.

Basic Components

AppCraft offers a variety of basic components that you can use to create the basic structure of your app. These components include buttons, labels, text fields, images, and more. Buttons allow users to interact with your app by tapping on them, labels are used to display text, text fields enable users to input text, and images can be used to enhance the visual appeal of your app. These basic components are the building blocks of your app's user interface.

Layout Components

Layout components in AppCraft are used to organize and structure the user interface of your app. These components include containers, grids, and stacks. Containers are used to group other components together, while grids and stacks provide a way to arrange components in a structured manner. Grids allow you to create a grid-like layout with rows and columns, while stacks enable you to stack components vertically or horizontally. By using layout components effectively, you can create visually appealing and user-friendly app interfaces.

Navigation Components

Navigation components in AppCraft are used to create navigation within your app. These components include screens, tabs, and menus. Screens represent different sections or pages of your app, tabs allow users to switch between different screens, and menus provide a way to access different app features or options. By using navigation components, you can create a seamless and intuitive navigation experience for your app users.

Data Components

Data components in AppCraft are used to fetch, display, and manipulate data within your app. These components include data sources, lists, and forms. Data sources are used to connect your app to external data sources such as databases or APIs. Lists allow you to display data in a list format, while forms enable users to input and submit data. By using data components effectively, you can create dynamic and interactive app experiences.

Media Components

Media components in AppCraft are used to incorporate media elements into your app. These components include audio players, video players, and image galleries. Audio players allow you to play audio files within your app, video players enable you to play video files, and image galleries provide a way to display multiple images in a slideshow format. By using media components, you can enhance the multimedia capabilities of your app.

Advanced Components

AppCraft also offers a range of advanced components that can be used to add advanced functionality to your app. These components include maps, charts, social media integrations, and more. Maps allow you to integrate maps and location-based services into your app, charts enable you to visualize data in a graphical format, and social media integrations provide a way to connect your app with popular social media platforms. By using advanced components, you can create feature-rich and engaging app experiences.

Custom Components

In addition to the pre-built components provided by AppCraft, you also have the ability to create your own custom components. Custom components allow you to create unique and specialized functionality that is tailored to the specific needs of your app. By using custom components, you can extend the capabilities of AppCraft and create truly unique and innovative apps.

Component Properties and Events

Each component in AppCraft has its own set of properties and events that you can customize and interact with. Properties define the characteristics and appearance of a component, while events allow you to respond to user interactions or system events. By understanding the properties and events of each component, you can fully leverage their capabilities and create dynamic and interactive app experiences.

In this section, we have explored the different types of components available in AppCraft and how you can use them to build your app. By understanding these components and their capabilities, you will be able to create visually appealing, user-friendly, and feature-rich apps using AppCraft.

3. Designing Your App

Planning Your App's User Interface

When it comes to building an app, one of the most crucial aspects is designing a user interface (UI) that is intuitive, visually appealing, and functional. The user interface is what users interact with when using your app, so it's essential to plan it carefully to ensure a positive user experience. In this section, we will explore the process of planning your app's user interface and discuss some best practices to consider.

Understanding User-Centered Design

Before diving into the specifics of planning your app's user interface, it's important to understand the concept of user-centered design. User-centered design is an approach that focuses on designing products or systems with the end-user in mind. It involves understanding the needs, goals, and preferences of your target audience and creating an interface that caters to those needs.

To begin the planning process, you should conduct user research to gain insights into your target audience. This can be done through surveys, interviews, or usability testing. By understanding your users' preferences, behaviors, and pain points, you can design an interface that meets their expectations and provides a seamless user experience.

Defining App Goals and Objectives

Before you start designing your app's user interface, it's important to define the goals and objectives of your app. What problem does your app solve? What value does it provide to users? By clearly defining your app's purpose, you can align your UI design with its goals.

Start by identifying the key features and functionalities your app will offer. This will help you determine the layout and structure of your user interface. Consider the flow of the app and how users will navigate through different screens and interact with various elements.

Sketching and Wireframing

Once you have a clear understanding of your app's goals and objectives, it's time to start sketching and wireframing your user interface. Sketching is a quick and low-fidelity way to explore different design ideas and layouts. It allows you to visualize the overall structure of your app and the placement of different elements.

Wireframing, on the other hand, is a more detailed representation of your app's user interface. It involves creating a visual blueprint of each screen, including the placement of buttons, text fields, images, and other interactive elements. Wireframes help you refine the layout and ensure that the user interface is logical and easy to navigate.

There are several tools available for sketching and wireframing, ranging from simple pen and paper to digital tools like Sketch, Figma, or Adobe XD. Choose a tool that suits your preferences and allows you to iterate quickly on your design ideas.

Considering Visual Hierarchy and Layout

When designing your app's user interface, it's important to consider visual hierarchy and layout. Visual hierarchy refers to the arrangement and prioritization of elements based on their importance. By using visual cues such as size, color, and typography, you can guide users' attention and make it easier for them to understand the content and functionality of your app.

Consider the layout of your app and how different elements will be organized on each screen. Use grids or columns to create a consistent and balanced layout. Pay attention to spacing between elements to ensure readability and avoid clutter. Remember to design for different screen sizes and orientations to provide a seamless experience across devices.

Choosing Colors, Fonts, and Images

Colors, fonts, and images play a significant role in creating a visually appealing user interface. Choose a color scheme that aligns with your app's branding and evokes the desired emotions. Consider the psychology of colors and how different colors can impact users' perception and behavior.

Select fonts that are legible and appropriate for your app's content. Use font styles and sizes to differentiate between headings, body text, and interactive elements. Consider the accessibility of your chosen fonts and ensure that they are readable for users with visual impairments.

Images and graphics can enhance the visual appeal of your app and provide context to users. Use high-quality images that are relevant to your app's content and purpose. Optimize images for different screen resolutions to ensure fast loading times.

Iterating and Gathering Feedback

Designing a user interface is an iterative process. Once you have created your initial sketches or wireframes, gather feedback from users, stakeholders, or other designers. This feedback can help you identify areas for improvement and refine your design.

Consider conducting usability testing to observe how users interact with your app's interface. This can provide valuable insights into usability issues and help you make informed design decisions. Iterate on your design based on the feedback received, and continue testing and refining until you achieve a user-friendly and visually appealing interface.

Documenting Your Design

As you progress through the planning and design process, it's important to document your design decisions. Create a style guide or design documentation that outlines the visual elements, color palette, typography, and other design guidelines for your app. This documentation will serve as a reference for developers and designers working on the implementation of your app.

By planning your app's user interface carefully and considering the needs and preferences of your target audience, you can create an engaging and intuitive app that users will love. Remember to iterate, gather feedback, and refine your design to ensure a seamless user experience.

Creating App Layouts and Screens

Once you have planned your app's user interface in the previous section, it's time to bring your design to life by creating app layouts and screens. In this section, we will explore the process of creating visually appealing and user-friendly app layouts using AppCraft.

Understanding App Layouts

An app layout refers to the arrangement of user interface elements such as buttons, text fields, images, and other components on the screen. A well-designed layout plays a crucial role in providing a seamless user experience and ensuring that your app looks professional and polished.

When creating app layouts, it's important to consider the following factors:

1. Screen Size and Orientation

Different devices have varying screen sizes and orientations. It's essential to design your app layouts to be responsive and adaptable to different screen sizes and orientations. AppCraft provides tools and features that allow you to create layouts that automatically adjust based on the device's screen size.

2. User Interaction

Consider how users will interact with your app and design your layouts accordingly. For example, if your app requires users to input text, you need to include text fields or input boxes in your layout. If your app involves navigation, you should include buttons or menus to facilitate easy navigation between screens.

3. Visual Hierarchy

Visual hierarchy refers to the arrangement and prioritization of elements on the screen. It helps users understand the importance and relationship between different elements. By using techniques such as size, color, and positioning, you can guide users' attention to the most important elements on the screen.

Creating App Screens

In AppCraft, you can create app screens by using a drag-and-drop interface. Here's a step-by-step guide on how to create app screens:

Step 1: Open the AppCraft Interface

Launch AppCraft and open your project. You will be greeted with the main interface, which consists of a canvas area where you can design your app screens.

Step 2: Add a New Screen

To add a new screen, click on the "Add Screen" button or select "New Screen" from the menu. Give your screen a name that reflects its purpose or functionality.

Step 3: Design the Layout

Once you have added a new screen, you can start designing its layout. AppCraft provides a wide range of pre-designed components that you can drag and drop onto the canvas. These components include buttons, text fields, images, labels, and more.

To add a component, simply drag it from the component library and drop it onto the canvas. You can then resize and position the component as desired. Use guidelines and alignment tools to ensure that your layout is visually balanced and aligned.

Step 4: Customize the Components

After adding components to your layout, you can customize their appearance and behavior. AppCraft allows you to change properties such as color, font, size, and alignment. You can also add interactions and animations to make your app more engaging and interactive.

Step 5: Connect Screens

If your app requires multiple screens, you can connect them using navigation components such as buttons or menus. By defining the navigation flow between screens, you can create a seamless user experience. AppCraft provides an intuitive interface for setting up screen transitions and navigation logic.

Step 6: Preview and Test

Once you have designed your app screens, it's important to preview and test them to ensure that they function as intended. AppCraft allows you to preview your app on different devices and screen sizes, allowing you to see how your layout adapts to different screen resolutions.

Best Practices for App Layouts

To create effective and visually appealing app layouts, consider the following best practices:

1. Keep it Simple

Simplicity is key when it comes to app layouts. Avoid cluttering the screen with too many elements or excessive text. Use white space effectively to create a clean and uncluttered design.

2. Consistency is Key

Maintain consistency in your app layouts to provide a cohesive user experience. Use consistent colors, fonts, and styles throughout your app. This helps users navigate your app more easily and creates a sense of familiarity.

3. Use Visual Cues

Use visual cues such as icons, buttons, and colors to guide users and indicate interactive elements. Visual cues help users understand how to interact with your app and improve the overall user experience.

4. Test and Iterate

Don't be afraid to test your app layouts with real users and gather feedback. User testing can help you identify areas for improvement and refine your layouts. Iterate on your designs based on user feedback to create a more user-friendly app.

By following these best practices and utilizing the features and tools provided by AppCraft, you can create visually appealing and user-friendly app layouts that enhance the overall user experience of your app.

In the next section, we will explore how to add colors, fonts, and images to your app to further enhance its visual appeal.

Adding Colors, Fonts, and Images

In this section, we will explore how to enhance the visual appeal of your app by adding colors, fonts, and images. These elements play a crucial role in creating an engaging and aesthetically pleasing user interface. By carefully selecting the right colors, fonts, and images, you can effectively communicate your app's brand identity and improve the overall user experience.

Choosing Colors

Colors have a significant impact on how users perceive and interact with your app. They can evoke emotions, convey meaning, and create a sense of harmony or contrast. When choosing colors for your app, it's essential to consider your target audience, the purpose of your app, and your brand identity.

Color Psychology

Different colors have different psychological effects on people. For example, warm colors like red, orange, and yellow can create a sense of energy and excitement, while cool colors like blue and green can evoke feelings of calmness and relaxation.

Understanding color psychology can help you select the right colors to convey the desired mood and message in your app.

Color Schemes

To create a visually appealing app, it's crucial to choose a harmonious color scheme. A color scheme is a set of colors that work well together and create a cohesive look and feel. Some popular color schemes include monochromatic (using different shades of a single color), complementary (using colors opposite each other on the color wheel), and analogous (using colors adjacent to each other on the color wheel).

Color Accessibility

When designing your app, it's essential to consider color accessibility for users with visual impairments. Ensure that the color contrast between text and background is sufficient to ensure readability. There are online tools available that can help you check the contrast ratio and ensure compliance with accessibility guidelines.

Selecting Fonts

Fonts play a crucial role in the readability and overall visual appeal of your app. When selecting fonts, it's important to consider legibility, brand consistency, and the overall tone of your app.

Font Categories

Fonts can be broadly categorized into serif, sans-serif, and display fonts. Serif fonts have small decorative lines at the ends of characters and are often associated with a more traditional and formal look. Sans-serif fonts, on the other hand, have clean lines and are commonly used for a modern and minimalist aesthetic. Display fonts are more decorative and are often used for headings and titles to create a unique and eye-catching look.

Font Pairing

To create a visually pleasing app, it's important to choose fonts that complement each other. Font pairing involves selecting two or more fonts that work well together and create a harmonious visual hierarchy. Typically, it's recommended to pair a serif font with a sans-serif font to create contrast and balance.

Font Sizes and Hierarchy

When designing your app's user interface, it's important to consider font sizes and hierarchy. Use larger font sizes for headings and important elements to draw attention, and smaller font sizes for body text and less significant information. Establishing a clear hierarchy through font sizes helps users navigate and understand the content of your app more easily.

Incorporating Images

Images are a powerful tool for conveying information, evoking emotions, and enhancing the visual appeal of your app. When incorporating images into your app, it's important to consider their purpose, quality, and relevance.

Image Types

There are various types of images you can use in your app, including photographs, illustrations, icons, and logos. Each type serves a different purpose and can be used to communicate specific information or create a particular visual style. For example, photographs can be used to showcase products or real-life scenarios, while icons can be used to represent actions or features.

Image Quality

To ensure a professional and polished look, it's important to use high-quality images in your app. Avoid using low-resolution or pixelated images, as they can negatively impact the overall user experience. If you're using photographs, consider using high-resolution images that are properly optimized for mobile devices.

Image Relevance

When selecting images for your app, it's crucial to choose ones that are relevant to your content and align with your app's purpose and brand identity. Images should enhance the user experience and provide visual cues that help users understand the app's functionality or content. Adding colors, fonts, and images to your app is an essential part of creating a visually appealing and engaging user interface. By carefully selecting colors that convey the desired mood, fonts that enhance readability and brand consistency, and images that are relevant and high-quality, you can create an app that stands out and captivates your users. Remember to consider color accessibility and font hierarchy to ensure a user-friendly experience. In the next section, we will explore how to implement app navigation to enhance the usability of your app.

Implementing App Navigation

App navigation is a crucial aspect of app design that determines how users move through different screens and sections of your app. It plays a significant role in providing a seamless and intuitive user experience. In this section, we will explore various techniques and best practices for implementing app navigation using AppCraft.

Understanding App Navigation Patterns

Before diving into the implementation details, it's essential to understand different app navigation patterns commonly used in mobile app design. Here are a few popular navigation patterns:

1. **Tab Bar Navigation**: This pattern involves placing a tab bar at the bottom of the screen, allowing users to switch between different sections or views of the app by tapping on the corresponding tabs. It is commonly used for apps with multiple primary sections or features.

2. **Drawer Navigation**: In this pattern, a navigation drawer or sidebar is used to display a list of app sections or categories. Users can open the drawer by swiping from the left edge of the screen or tapping on a menu icon. It is suitable for apps with a large number of sections or settings.

3. **Stacked Navigation**: Stacked navigation involves maintaining a stack of screens or views, where users can navigate back and forth by pushing and popping screens from the stack. It is commonly used for apps with a linear

flow, such as signup or onboarding processes.

4. **Modal Navigation**: Modal navigation displays a temporary screen or view on top of the current screen, typically used for tasks that require user input or confirmation. Users can dismiss the modal by tapping outside the modal or using a close button.

5. **Tabbed Navigation**: Tabbed navigation is similar to tab bar navigation but uses tabs placed at the top of the screen instead of the bottom. It is commonly used for apps with a smaller number of primary sections.

Implementing Navigation in AppCraft

AppCraft provides a range of tools and components to implement app navigation efficiently. Let's explore some of the key features and techniques for implementing navigation in your app:

1. **Navigation Bar**: The navigation bar is a common component used to display the app's title, navigation buttons, and other relevant information. AppCraft allows you to customize the navigation bar's appearance and add buttons for common actions such as back, home, or search.

2. **Screen Transitions**: AppCraft offers various screen transition animations to enhance the user experience when navigating between screens. You can choose from options like slide, fade, or flip animations to create visually appealing transitions.

3. **Navigation Actions**: AppCraft provides a set of built-in navigation actions that allow you to navigate between screens programmatically. You can use actions like "Push Screen," "Pop Screen," or "Present Modal" to control the flow of your app.

4. **Navigation Variables**: AppCraft allows you to define navigation variables that can be used to pass data between screens. For example, you can pass user information from a

login screen to a profile screen using navigation variables.

5. **Conditional Navigation**: With AppCraft, you can implement conditional navigation based on certain conditions or user interactions. For example, you can navigate to a different screen based on the user's role or permissions.

Best Practices for App Navigation

To ensure a smooth and intuitive navigation experience for your app users, consider the following best practices:

1. **Consistency**: Maintain consistency in your app's navigation patterns and design elements across different screens. This helps users understand and predict how to navigate through your app.

2. **Simplicity**: Keep your app's navigation simple and straightforward. Avoid overwhelming users with too many options or complex navigation flows. Focus on providing a clear and concise navigation structure.

3. **Hierarchy**: Organize your app's navigation hierarchy in a logical and hierarchical manner. Group related screens or sections together to make it easier for users to find what they are looking for.

4. **Feedback**: Provide visual feedback to users when they interact with navigation elements. For example, highlight the selected tab or change the color of a button when tapped. This helps users understand their current location within the app.

5. **User Testing**: Conduct user testing to gather feedback on your app's navigation. Observe how users navigate through your app and identify any pain points or areas of confusion. Use this feedback to refine and improve your app's navigation.

Implementing effective app navigation is crucial for creating a user-friendly and engaging app. AppCraft provides a range of tools and techniques to help you implement navigation patterns that suit your app's requirements. By following best practices and considering user feedback, you can create a seamless navigation experience that enhances the overall usability of your app. In the next section, we will explore how to enhance the user experience with animations in AppCraft.

Enhancing User Experience with Animations

Animations play a crucial role in enhancing the user experience of an app. They can make the app feel more dynamic, engaging, and intuitive. In this section, we will explore the different types of animations you can incorporate into your app using AppCraft, and how to implement them effectively.

Understanding the Importance of Animations

Animations are not just eye candy; they serve a purpose in improving the overall user experience. Here are a few reasons why animations are important in app design:

1. **Visual Feedback**: Animations provide visual cues to users, indicating that an action has been performed or a transition is taking place. This feedback helps users understand the app's response to their interactions, making the app feel more responsive and intuitive.

2. **Guiding User Attention**: Animations can direct the user's attention to important elements or changes within the app. By using animations strategically, you can guide users through the app's interface and highlight key features or information.

3. **Smooth Transitions**: Animations can make transitions between screens or views appear seamless and smooth. This creates a more polished and professional feel, reducing any jarring or abrupt changes that may disrupt the user's

flow.

4. **Delightful User Experience**: Well-designed animations can add an element of delight and surprise to the user experience. They can make the app feel more enjoyable and memorable, leaving a positive impression on users.

Types of Animations

AppCraft provides various animation options that you can use to enhance your app's user experience. Let's explore some of the most commonly used types of animations:

1. **Transition Animations**: These animations are used to create smooth transitions between different screens or views within the app. Examples include fade-ins, slide-ins, and cross-fades. Transition animations help users understand the spatial relationships between different app elements and provide a sense of continuity.

2. **Microinteractions**: Microinteractions are small, subtle animations that occur in response to user actions. They provide immediate feedback and create a sense of direct manipulation. Examples include button press animations, loading spinners, and progress bars. Microinteractions make the app feel more responsive and engaging.

3. **Scrolling Animations**: Scrolling animations are used to add visual interest and interactivity to scrolling content. Parallax effects, where different layers of content move at different speeds, can create a sense of depth and immersion. Additionally, scroll-triggered animations can be used to reveal or hide elements as the user scrolls through the app.

4. **Gestural Animations**: Gestural animations respond to specific user gestures, such as swipes, pinches, or taps. These animations provide visual feedback and help users understand the cause and effect relationship between their actions and the app's response. For example, a swipe gesture can trigger a card flip animation or a pinch gesture

can zoom in or out of an image.

5. **Loading Animations**: Loading animations are used to indicate that the app is processing or retrieving data. They help manage user expectations and reduce perceived waiting time. Loading animations can take the form of spinners, progress bars, or skeleton screens. It's important to strike a balance between providing feedback and not making the user feel impatient.

Implementing Animations in AppCraft

AppCraft provides a user-friendly interface for implementing animations in your app. Here are the steps to follow:

1. **Identify Animation Opportunities**: Start by identifying areas in your app where animations can enhance the user experience. Consider transitions between screens, button interactions, scrolling effects, and any other areas where animations can provide visual feedback or improve the flow.

2. **Choose Animation Types**: Select the appropriate animation types based on the identified opportunities. Consider the purpose of the animation and how it aligns with your app's overall design and branding.

3. **Configure Animation Properties**: AppCraft allows you to customize various properties of animations, such as duration, easing, delay, and direction. Experiment with different settings to achieve the desired effect.

4. **Apply Animations to Elements**: Use AppCraft's intuitive interface to apply animations to specific elements within your app. This can be done through drag-and-drop or by selecting the desired elements and applying the animations from the properties panel.

5. **Preview and Refine**: Preview the animations within AppCraft to see how they look and feel. Make any necessary adjustments to the animation properties or timing to ensure a

smooth and visually appealing experience.

6. **Test on Different Devices**: Test your app on different devices to ensure that the animations work well across various screen sizes and resolutions. Pay attention to performance and ensure that the animations do not negatively impact the app's responsiveness.

Best Practices for Using Animations

To make the most of animations in your app, consider the following best practices:

1. **Keep it Subtle**: Avoid overwhelming the user with excessive or flashy animations. Subtle animations that enhance the user experience without being distracting are often more effective.

2. **Consistency is Key**: Maintain consistency in your animation styles and timings throughout the app. This creates a cohesive and familiar experience for users.

3. **Consider Performance**: While animations can greatly enhance the user experience, they can also impact app performance if not implemented properly. Optimize your animations to ensure smooth performance on different devices.

4. **User Control**: Provide options for users to control or disable animations if they prefer. Some users may have visual impairments or simply prefer a more static experience.

5. **Test and Iterate**: Test your animations with real users and gather feedback to identify areas for improvement. Iterate on your animations based on user feedback to create the best possible user experience.

By incorporating well-designed animations into your app, you can create a more engaging and delightful user experience. Experiment with different animation types and techniques to find the perfect balance that aligns with your app's purpose and target audience.

Testing and Refining Your App Design

Once you have designed the user interface and implemented the necessary features and functionalities in your app, it is crucial to thoroughly test and refine your app design. Testing helps identify any issues or bugs in your app, while refining allows you to make improvements and enhancements to ensure a seamless user experience. In this section, we will explore the importance of testing and refining your app design and discuss some best practices to follow.

Importance of Testing Your App Design

Testing your app design is a critical step in the app development process. It allows you to identify and fix any issues or bugs before releasing your app to the users. By thoroughly testing your app, you can ensure that it functions as intended and provides a smooth and error-free experience to your users. Here are some reasons why testing is important:

1. **Bug Identification**: Testing helps you identify any bugs or errors in your app's functionality, ensuring that it works as expected. By catching and fixing these issues early on, you can prevent potential problems and improve the overall quality of your app.

2. **User Experience Enhancement**: Testing allows you to evaluate the user experience of your app. By gathering feedback from testers, you can identify areas where the user interface can be improved, making it more intuitive and user-friendly.

3. **Compatibility Testing**: Testing helps ensure that your app works seamlessly across different devices, operating systems, and screen sizes. By conducting compatibility testing, you can identify any issues specific to certain platforms and make the necessary adjustments to provide a

consistent experience to all users.

4. **Performance Optimization**: Testing helps you identify any performance issues in your app, such as slow loading times or crashes. By optimizing the performance of your app, you can provide a smooth and responsive experience to your users, enhancing their satisfaction and engagement.

Types of Testing

There are various types of testing that you can perform to ensure the quality and functionality of your app. Let's explore some common types of testing:

1. **Functional Testing**: This type of testing focuses on verifying that each function of your app works correctly. It involves testing individual features and functionalities to ensure they perform as intended.

2. **Usability Testing**: Usability testing evaluates the user-friendliness of your app. It involves observing users as they interact with your app and gathering feedback on its ease of use, navigation, and overall user experience.

3. **Compatibility Testing**: Compatibility testing ensures that your app works seamlessly across different devices, browsers, and operating systems. It involves testing your app on various platforms to identify any compatibility issues and make the necessary adjustments.

4. **Performance Testing**: Performance testing evaluates the speed, responsiveness, and stability of your app. It involves testing your app under different conditions to identify any performance bottlenecks and optimize its performance.

5. **Security Testing**: Security testing focuses on identifying any vulnerabilities or weaknesses in your app's security. It involves testing your app for potential security breaches and implementing measures to protect user data.

Best Practices for Testing and Refining Your App Design

To ensure the effectiveness of your testing and refining process, it is essential to follow some best practices. Here are some tips to consider:

1. **Create a Testing Plan**: Before starting the testing process, create a detailed plan outlining the different types of testing you will perform, the devices and platforms you will test on, and the expected outcomes. This will help you stay organized and ensure comprehensive testing coverage.

2. **Test Early and Often**: Start testing your app as early as possible in the development process. This allows you to catch and fix issues early on, saving time and effort in the long run. Additionally, perform regular testing throughout the development process to ensure that new features and changes do not introduce any new issues.

3. **Use Real-World Scenarios**: When testing your app, simulate real-world scenarios to ensure that it performs well in different situations. Consider factors such as slow internet connections, low battery levels, and multitasking to evaluate the app's performance and responsiveness.

4. **Involve Beta Testers**: Engage a group of beta testers to test your app before its official release. Beta testers can provide valuable feedback and help identify any issues or areas for improvement that you may have overlooked. Encourage them to provide detailed feedback and report any bugs they encounter.

5. **Monitor and Analyze User Feedback**: Once your app is released, monitor user feedback and reviews to identify any issues or areas for improvement. Actively engage with your users and address their concerns promptly. Analyze user behavior and usage patterns to gain insights into how users interact with your app and make data-driven decisions for further refinements.

6. **Iterate and Improve**: Use the feedback and insights gathered from testing to iterate and improve your app design. Continuously refine your app based on user feedback, market trends, and emerging technologies to stay ahead of the competition and provide an exceptional user experience.

By following these best practices, you can ensure that your app design is thoroughly tested and refined, resulting in a high-quality and user-friendly app.

In the next chapter, we will explore the process of working with data in your app, including understanding data models, creating and managing data sources, and fetching and displaying data.

This concludes section 3.6 on testing and refining your app design. Testing is a crucial step in the app development process, allowing you to identify and fix any issues or bugs before releasing your app to the users. By following best practices and thoroughly testing your app, you can ensure a seamless user experience and improve the overall quality of your app.

4. Working with Data

Understanding Data Models

In the world of app development, data is at the core of every application. Whether it's user information, product details, or any other type of data, understanding how to work with data models is essential. Data models define the structure and relationships of the data within an application, allowing developers to organize and manipulate information effectively.

What is a Data Model?

A data model is a conceptual representation of the data that an application will store and manipulate. It defines the structure, attributes, and relationships of the data entities within the application. Think of it as a blueprint that guides the development process and ensures consistency and integrity in handling data.

Data models can take different forms depending on the app's requirements and the chosen development approach. Some common types of data models include:

1. **Relational Data Model**: This model organizes data into tables with rows and columns, where each table represents an entity, and the columns represent attributes. Relationships between entities are established through keys, such as primary keys and foreign keys.

2. **Object-Oriented Data Model**: In this model, data is represented as objects with properties and methods. Objects can have relationships with other objects, allowing for complex data structures.

3. **Document Data Model**: This model stores data in a document format, such as JSON or XML. Documents can contain nested structures, making it suitable for handling unstructured or semi-structured data.

4. **Graph Data Model**: This model represents data as nodes and edges, where nodes represent entities, and edges represent relationships between entities. It is particularly useful for modeling complex relationships and networks.

Designing a Data Model

Designing a data model involves identifying the entities, attributes, and relationships that will be part of the application's data structure. Here are the key steps involved in designing a data model:

1. **Identify Entities**: Start by identifying the main entities or objects that will be part of your application. For example, if you are building an e-commerce app, entities could include customers, products, orders, and reviews.

2. **Define Attributes**: For each entity, define the attributes or properties that describe it. For example, a customer entity may have attributes like name, email, and address. These attributes will determine the type of data that needs to be stored.

3. **Establish Relationships**: Determine the relationships between entities. Relationships can be one-to-one, one-to-many, or many-to-many. For example, a customer can have multiple orders, and an order can have multiple products.

4. **Normalize Data**: Normalize the data model to eliminate redundancy and ensure data integrity. This involves breaking down entities into smaller, more manageable tables and establishing relationships between them.

5. **Consider Performance**: Consider the performance implications of your data model. Optimize it for efficient data retrieval and manipulation. This may involve denormalizing certain parts of the model or using indexing techniques.

Implementing Data Models

Once the data model is designed, it needs to be implemented in the chosen app building software. The implementation process may vary depending on the software you are using, but here are some general steps to follow:

1. **Create Tables or Classes**: In relational databases, you will create tables that correspond to the entities in your data model. Each table will have columns representing the attributes. In object-oriented programming, you will create classes that represent the entities, with properties representing the attributes.

2. **Define Relationships**: Establish relationships between tables or classes. In relational databases, this involves defining primary and foreign keys to establish relationships between tables. In object-oriented programming, you can use object references or collections to represent

relationships.

3. **Map Attributes**: Map the attributes of your entities to the appropriate columns or properties. This ensures that the data is stored and retrieved correctly.

4. **Implement Data Validation**: Implement data validation rules to ensure that the data being stored meets the defined criteria. This helps maintain data integrity and prevents errors.

5. **Implement Data Access**: Implement the necessary code or queries to access and manipulate the data. This may involve writing SQL queries, using object-relational mapping frameworks, or using built-in data access methods provided by the app building software.

Data Modeling Best Practices

To ensure a robust and efficient data model, consider the following best practices:

1. **Simplicity**: Keep the data model as simple as possible. Avoid unnecessary complexity that can lead to confusion and performance issues.

2. **Normalization**: Normalize the data model to eliminate redundancy and ensure data integrity. This helps maintain consistency and reduces the chances of data anomalies.

3. **Scalability**: Design the data model with scalability in mind. Consider future growth and potential changes in data requirements.

4. **Flexibility**: Design the data model to be flexible and adaptable to changes. Anticipate possible modifications or additions to the data structure.

5. **Documentation**: Document the data model thoroughly. This helps in understanding the structure and relationships of the

data, especially for future maintenance or updates.

By understanding data models and following best practices, you can create a solid foundation for your app's data structure. A well-designed data model ensures efficient data management, enhances performance, and allows for easier maintenance and scalability.

Creating and Managing Data Sources

In order to create a fully functional app, it is essential to work with data. Data sources are the backbone of any app, as they provide the information that the app needs to function properly. In this section, we will explore how to create and manage data sources in AppCraft.

Understanding Data Sources

Before we dive into creating data sources, let's first understand what they are. In simple terms, a data source is a location where your app can retrieve and store data. This data can come from various sources such as databases, APIs, or even local storage on the user's device.

Data sources can be categorized into two types: local and remote. Local data sources are stored directly on the user's device, while remote data sources are accessed over the internet. Depending on the requirements of your app, you may need to work with one or both types of data sources.

Creating Local Data Sources

Local data sources are commonly used when you need to store and retrieve data on the user's device. AppCraft provides several options for creating and managing local data sources.

Using Local Storage

One of the simplest ways to create a local data source is by using the local storage feature provided by AppCraft. Local storage allows you to store data on the user's device, which can be accessed even when the app is offline.

To create a local data source using local storage, you can follow these steps:

1. Open the AppCraft interface and navigate to the "Data" section.
2. Click on the "Add Data Source" button.
3. Select "Local Storage" as the data source type.
4. Provide a name for your data source and specify any additional settings.
5. Save the data source.

Once you have created a local data source, you can start storing and retrieving data from it using AppCraft's built-in functions and actions.

Working with Databases

If your app requires more complex data storage and retrieval capabilities, you can consider using a database as your local data source. AppCraft supports various database options, including SQLite and Firebase.

To create a database data source, you will need to follow these steps:

1. Open the AppCraft interface and navigate to the "Data" section.
2. Click on the "Add Data Source" button.
3. Select the type of database you want to use (e.g., SQLite or Firebase).
4. Provide the necessary credentials and connection details for the database.
5. Save the data source.

Once you have created a database data source, you can use SQL queries or AppCraft's database actions to interact with the data stored in the database.

Creating Remote Data Sources

Remote data sources are essential when your app needs to fetch data from external APIs or web services. AppCraft provides several options for creating and managing remote data sources.

RESTful APIs

RESTful APIs are a popular choice for integrating external data sources into your app. These APIs allow you to send HTTP requests to a server and receive data in a structured format, such as JSON or XML.

To create a remote data source using a RESTful API, you can follow these steps:

1. Open the AppCraft interface and navigate to the "Data" section.
2. Click on the "Add Data Source" button.
3. Select "RESTful API" as the data source type.
4. Provide the URL of the API and any necessary authentication details.
5. Save the data source.

Once you have created a remote data source, you can use AppCraft's API actions to send requests to the API and retrieve the data.

Web Services

In addition to RESTful APIs, AppCraft also supports integration with various web services. These services provide specific functionalities, such as user authentication or real-time data updates.

To create a remote data source using a web service, you will typically need to follow the service's documentation and guidelines. AppCraft provides specific actions and components for popular web services, making the integration process easier.

Managing Data Sources

Once you have created data sources in AppCraft, it is important to manage them effectively. Managing data sources involves tasks such as updating data, handling data synchronization, and ensuring data security.

Updating Data

As your app evolves, you may need to update the data stored in your data sources. AppCraft provides various methods for updating data, depending on the type of data source you are working with.

For local data sources, you can use AppCraft's built-in functions and actions to update the data directly. For example, you can use the "Set Value" action to update a specific value in a local data source.

For remote data sources, you will typically need to use the appropriate API or web service actions provided by AppCraft. These actions allow you to send requests to the data source and update the data accordingly.

Data Synchronization

In some cases, your app may need to synchronize data between different devices or users. AppCraft provides features and actions to facilitate data synchronization, ensuring that all users have access to the most up-to-date information.

For local data sources, you can use AppCraft's synchronization actions to handle data synchronization. These actions allow you to define synchronization rules and specify how conflicts should be resolved.

For remote data sources, synchronization is typically handled by the API or web service itself. You will need to follow the documentation and guidelines provided by the service to implement data synchronization.

Data Security

Data security is a critical aspect of app development. AppCraft provides various features and options to ensure the security of your data sources.

For local data sources, you can implement encryption and access control mechanisms to protect the data stored on the user's device.

AppCraft provides built-in functions and actions for implementing these security measures.

For remote data sources, data security is typically handled by the API or web service. You will need to follow the security guidelines provided by the service to ensure the confidentiality and integrity of your data. Creating and managing data sources is a crucial step in app development. By understanding the different types of data sources and how to work with them in AppCraft, you can effectively store, retrieve, and update data in your app. Whether you are working with local or remote data sources, AppCraft provides the necessary tools and actions to make the process seamless. In the next section, we will explore how to fetch and display data in your app.

Fetching and Displaying Data

In order to create dynamic and interactive apps, it is crucial to understand how to fetch and display data. Whether you need to retrieve information from a remote server, a local database, or an API, this section will guide you through the process of fetching and displaying data in your AppCraft applications.

Understanding Data Sources

Before we dive into the specifics of fetching and displaying data, it is important to understand the concept of data sources. A data source is a location where your app retrieves information from. This can include databases, APIs, web services, or even local storage.

When working with data sources, it is essential to consider factors such as data security, reliability, and performance. Depending on the nature of your app and the type of data you need to fetch, you may choose different data sources. For example, if you are building an e-commerce app, you might fetch product information from an API provided by your backend server.

Fetching Data

Fetching data involves making a request to a data source and retrieving the desired information. AppCraft provides various methods and components to facilitate this process.

Using HTTP Requests

One common way to fetch data is by making HTTP requests. AppCraft offers built-in components that allow you to send GET, POST, PUT, and DELETE requests to a server. These components handle the communication with the server and provide you with the response data.

To fetch data using HTTP requests, you need to specify the URL of the server endpoint and the desired HTTP method. You can also include parameters, headers, and a request body if necessary. Once the request is sent, you can handle the response data and update your app accordingly.

Working with APIs

APIs (Application Programming Interfaces) are a common way to fetch data from external sources. They allow your app to communicate with other applications or services and retrieve specific information.

AppCraft provides components and methods to interact with APIs seamlessly. You can use the HTTP request components mentioned earlier to send requests to API endpoints. Additionally, you can parse the response data using JSON or XML parsing components to extract the relevant information.

When working with APIs, it is important to understand the authentication and authorization mechanisms required by the API provider. Some APIs may require an API key or authentication token to access the data. AppCraft provides components to handle these authentication processes, ensuring secure and authorized data retrieval.

Displaying Data

Once you have fetched the data, the next step is to display it in your app's user interface. AppCraft offers a wide range of components and techniques to present data in a visually appealing and user-friendly manner.

Using Data Binding

Data binding is a powerful feature that allows you to bind data directly to UI components. With data binding, you can automatically update the UI whenever the underlying data changes, eliminating the need for manual updates.

AppCraft provides data binding components that enable you to bind data from your data source to UI elements such as labels, text fields, images, and more. By establishing this connection, any changes in the data will be reflected in the UI, providing a seamless and dynamic user experience.

Creating Dynamic Lists

In many cases, you may need to display a list of items fetched from a data source. AppCraft offers components such as list views and collection views that allow you to create dynamic lists with ease.

By binding the list component to your data source, you can automatically populate the list with the fetched data. You can customize the appearance of each list item and handle user interactions such as tapping or swiping on individual items.

Formatting and Presenting Data

When displaying data, it is important to consider the formatting and presentation to ensure clarity and readability. AppCraft provides various formatting components that allow you to format data according to your app's requirements.

You can format dates, numbers, currencies, and other types of data using the provided formatting components. Additionally, you can customize the appearance of UI elements to present the data in a visually appealing manner. This includes changing fonts, colors, and styles to match your app's design.

Caching and Offline Support

In some scenarios, it may be beneficial to cache the fetched data to improve performance and provide offline support. Caching allows your app to store a copy of the fetched data locally, reducing the need for repeated network requests.

AppCraft provides caching mechanisms that enable you to store and retrieve data from local storage. By implementing caching, you can ensure that your app functions smoothly even when the device is offline or experiencing network connectivity issues.

Error Handling and Data Validation

When fetching and displaying data, it is important to handle errors and validate the retrieved data. AppCraft provides error handling components that allow you to handle various types of errors, such as network errors or server-side errors.

Additionally, you can implement data validation techniques to ensure the integrity and accuracy of the fetched data. This includes checking for missing or invalid data, validating data formats, and handling edge cases.

By implementing robust error handling and data validation mechanisms, you can provide a reliable and seamless user experience, even in the face of unexpected errors or data inconsistencies. Fetching and displaying data is a fundamental aspect of app development. By understanding the concepts and techniques discussed in this section, you will be able to create dynamic and interactive apps that retrieve and present data from various sources. Whether you are working with APIs, databases, or other data sources, AppCraft provides the necessary tools and components to simplify the process. In the next section, we will explore how to implement data validation and security measures to ensure the integrity and safety of your app's data.

Implementing Data Validation and Security

Data validation and security are crucial aspects of app development. In this section, we will explore the importance of implementing data validation and security measures in your app built with AppCraft. We will discuss various techniques and best practices to ensure that your app's data is validated, protected, and secure.

Understanding Data Validation

Data validation is the process of ensuring that the data entered into your app is accurate, complete, and conforms to the expected format. By implementing data validation, you can prevent errors, improve user experience, and protect your app from malicious activities.

Types of Data Validation

There are several types of data validation techniques that you can implement in your app:

1. **Presence Validation**: This type of validation ensures that a required field is not left empty. It checks if the user has entered data in all the mandatory fields.

2. **Format Validation**: Format validation ensures that the data entered matches the expected format. For example, if you have a field for email addresses, format validation will check if the entered value follows the standard email format.

3. **Range Validation**: Range validation checks if the entered value falls within a specified range. For example, if you have a field for age, range validation can ensure that the entered age is within a valid range, such as 18 to 99.

4. **Length Validation**: Length validation checks if the length of the entered value is within the specified limits. For example, if you have a field for a username, length validation can ensure that the entered username is not too short or too long.

5. **Pattern Validation**: Pattern validation checks if the entered value matches a specific pattern. This is useful when you want to enforce a specific format, such as phone numbers or postal codes.

Implementing Data Validation in AppCraft

AppCraft provides various tools and features to implement data validation in your app. Here are some steps to follow:

1. **Identify the Data to Validate**: Determine which fields in your app require data validation. This can include user input fields, form submissions, or data fetched from external sources.

2. **Choose the Validation Technique**: Select the appropriate validation technique based on the type of data you want to validate. For example, if you have a field for email addresses, you can use format validation to ensure that the entered value is a valid email address.

3. **Implement Validation Rules**: Use AppCraft's validation components and functions to define the validation rules for each field. You can specify the required format, range, length, or pattern for the data.

4. **Display Validation Errors**: When a user submits invalid data, display meaningful error messages to guide them on how to correct the errors. AppCraft provides built-in error handling mechanisms that you can utilize to display validation errors.

Ensuring Data Security

Data security is of utmost importance in app development, especially when dealing with sensitive user information. By implementing proper security measures, you can protect your app and its data from unauthorized access, data breaches, and other security threats.

Secure Data Storage

When storing data in your app, it is essential to ensure that it is securely stored and encrypted. AppCraft provides built-in features to securely store data, such as user credentials, personal information, and sensitive data. You can utilize encryption algorithms and secure storage mechanisms provided by AppCraft to protect the data stored in your app.

User Authentication and Authorization

Implementing user authentication and authorization is crucial to ensure that only authorized users can access certain features or data within your app. AppCraft offers various authentication methods, such as username/password authentication, social media login, or integration with third-party authentication providers. By implementing proper authentication and authorization mechanisms, you can protect user data and prevent unauthorized access.

Secure Network Communication

When your app communicates with external servers or APIs, it is essential to ensure that the network communication is secure. AppCraft supports secure network protocols, such as HTTPS, to encrypt the data transmitted between your app and the server. By using secure network communication, you can prevent eavesdropping, data tampering, and other security threats.

Regular Security Audits and Updates

To maintain the security of your app, it is crucial to perform regular security audits and updates. Stay updated with the latest security practices and vulnerabilities to identify and fix any security loopholes in your app. AppCraft regularly releases updates and security patches to address any security vulnerabilities, so make sure to keep your app up to date.

Best Practices for Data Validation and Security

To ensure effective data validation and security in your app, consider the following best practices:

1. **Validate All User Input**: Validate all user input to prevent malicious data from entering your app. Implement both client-side and server-side validation to ensure data integrity.

2. **Use Strong Password Policies**: If your app involves user accounts, enforce strong password policies to protect user

accounts from unauthorized access. Encourage users to create strong passwords and consider implementing additional security measures like two-factor authentication.

3. **Encrypt Sensitive Data**: Encrypt sensitive data, such as user credentials or personal information, when storing it in your app. Utilize encryption algorithms and secure storage mechanisms provided by AppCraft to protect the data.

4. **Implement Role-Based Access Control**: Implement role-based access control to restrict access to certain features or data based on user roles. This ensures that only authorized users can access sensitive information.

5. **Regularly Test for Vulnerabilities**: Perform regular security testing and vulnerability assessments to identify and fix any security loopholes in your app. Use security testing tools and techniques to ensure the robustness of your app's security measures.

By implementing data validation and security measures in your app built with AppCraft, you can ensure the integrity, confidentiality, and availability of your app's data. Protecting user data and maintaining a secure app environment is essential for building trust with your users and ensuring the success of your app.

5.Adding Functionality to Your App

Working with AppCraft Actions

In order to create a fully functional and interactive app, you need to understand how to work with actions in AppCraft. Actions are a fundamental part of app development as they allow you to define the behavior and functionality of your app. In this section, we will explore the various types of actions available in AppCraft and how to use them effectively.

Understanding AppCraft Actions

Actions in AppCraft are predefined functions or behaviors that can be triggered by events or user interactions. They allow you to add interactivity and functionality to your app without writing complex code. AppCraft provides a wide range of actions that cover common app functionalities such as button clicks, form submissions, data manipulation, and more.

Each action in AppCraft consists of two main components: the trigger and the action itself. The trigger is an event or user interaction that initiates the action, while the action defines what should happen when the trigger occurs. For example, you can set a button click as the trigger and define the action to navigate to another screen when the button is clicked.

Adding Actions to AppCraft Components

To add actions to your app, you need to associate them with specific components in your app's user interface. AppCraft provides a simple and intuitive interface for adding actions to components. Here's a step-by-step guide on how to add actions to AppCraft components:

1. Select the component you want to add an action to. This can be a button, a form field, a list item, or any other interactive component.

2. In the properties panel of the selected component, look for the "Actions" section. This is where you can define the actions associated with the component.

3. Click on the "Add Action" button to open the action editor. Here, you can choose the trigger for the action from a list of available options.

4. Once you have selected the trigger, you can define the action that should be performed when the trigger occurs. This can include navigating to another screen, submitting a

form, displaying a message, or any other desired functionality.

5. Customize the action parameters based on your app's requirements. For example, if you are navigating to another screen, you can specify the target screen or pass data between screens.

6. Save the action and repeat the process for other components in your app that require actions.

By adding actions to your app's components, you can create a dynamic and interactive user experience. Users can interact with your app by tapping buttons, filling out forms, or performing other actions, and the app will respond accordingly based on the defined actions.

Working with Action Conditions and Variables

AppCraft allows you to add conditions and variables to your actions, enabling you to create more complex and dynamic app behaviors. Conditions allow you to specify certain criteria that must be met for an action to be executed. For example, you can add a condition to a button click action that checks if a form field is filled out correctly before submitting the form.

Variables, on the other hand, allow you to store and manipulate data within your app. You can use variables to store user input, retrieve data from a database, or perform calculations. By combining conditions and variables, you can create powerful and flexible app functionalities.

To add conditions or variables to your actions in AppCraft, follow these steps:

1. Open the action editor for the desired action.

2. Look for the "Conditions" or "Variables" section in the action editor.

3. Add conditions or variables by clicking on the respective buttons and specifying the criteria or data you want to use.

4. Customize the conditions or variables based on your app's requirements.

By utilizing conditions and variables, you can create app behaviors that respond intelligently to user input and data changes. This allows you to build more sophisticated and personalized apps.

Testing and Debugging Actions

Once you have added actions to your app, it is important to thoroughly test and debug them to ensure they work as intended. AppCraft provides built-in testing and debugging tools that allow you to simulate user interactions and track the execution of actions.

To test and debug actions in AppCraft, follow these steps:

1. Use the preview mode in AppCraft to simulate user interactions and test the functionality of your app.

2. Monitor the execution of actions in real-time using the debugging console. The console provides valuable information about the actions being triggered, any errors that occur, and the flow of data within your app.

3. If you encounter any issues or errors, use the debugging console to identify the problem and make necessary adjustments to your actions.

By thoroughly testing and debugging your actions, you can ensure that your app functions correctly and provides a seamless user experience. Working with actions in AppCraft is essential for adding functionality and interactivity to your app. By understanding how to use actions effectively, you can create dynamic and engaging user experiences. In this section, we explored the different types of actions available in AppCraft, how to add actions to components, and how to work with action conditions and variables. We also discussed the importance of testing and debugging actions to ensure their proper functionality. With this knowledge, you are now equipped to create powerful and interactive apps using AppCraft.

Implementing User Input and Interactivity

In order to create a successful and engaging app, it is crucial to implement user input and interactivity. This allows users to actively engage with your app, providing them with a more personalized and interactive experience. In this section, we will explore various techniques and strategies for implementing user input and interactivity in your AppCraft app.

Capturing User Input

One of the fundamental aspects of user interactivity is capturing user input. This can include various forms of input such as text, numbers, selections, and more. AppCraft provides a range of components and actions that allow you to capture user input effectively.

Text Input Fields

Text input fields are commonly used to capture user input in the form of text. AppCraft provides a Text Input component that allows you to easily add text input fields to your app. You can customize the appearance and behavior of these fields, such as setting placeholder text, defining input restrictions, and handling user input events.

Buttons and Click Events

Buttons are another essential component for capturing user input. You can add buttons to your app and define click events that are triggered when the user taps on the button. These click events can be used to perform various actions, such as submitting a form, navigating to a different screen, or triggering a specific functionality within your app.

Selection Inputs

Selection inputs are useful when you want users to choose from a predefined set of options. AppCraft provides components like Dropdowns, Radio Buttons, and Checkboxes that allow you to implement selection inputs easily. You can define the available options and handle the user's selection using appropriate actions and event handlers.

Validating User Input

Validating user input is crucial to ensure that the data entered by the user meets the required criteria. AppCraft provides built-in validation actions and functions that allow you to validate user input effectively.

Required Fields

One common validation requirement is to ensure that certain fields are not left empty. You can use the "Required" validation action to check if a field has been filled by the user. If the field is empty, you can display an error message or prevent the user from proceeding until the required field is filled.

Format Validation

In addition to checking for required fields, you may also need to validate the format of the user's input. For example, you might want to ensure that an email address is entered correctly or that a phone number follows a specific format. AppCraft provides various validation actions and functions that allow you to validate input based on specific formats or patterns.

Custom Validation

Sometimes, the validation requirements of your app may be unique and not covered by the built-in validation actions. In such cases, you can implement custom validation logic using AppCraft's custom code feature. This allows you to write your own validation functions and actions to validate user input based on your specific requirements.

Responding to User Input

Once you have captured and validated user input, it is important to respond to it appropriately. This involves updating the app's interface, performing actions based on the user's input, and providing feedback to the user.

Updating App State

User input often triggers changes in the app's state or data. For example, when a user selects an option from a dropdown, you may need to update the displayed content based on the selected option. AppCraft provides actions and functions that allow you to update the app's state dynamically in response to user input.

Conditional Actions

In some cases, you may want to perform specific actions based on the user's input. For example, if a user selects a certain option, you may want to display additional fields or show/hide certain elements in the app. AppCraft allows you to define conditional actions that are triggered based on specific user input, enabling you to create dynamic and interactive app experiences.

Providing Feedback

Providing feedback to the user is essential for a smooth and intuitive user experience. AppCraft provides various components and actions that allow you to provide feedback to the user based on their input. This can include displaying success messages, error messages, or visual indicators to indicate the status of a particular action.

Enhancing Interactivity with Animations

Animations can greatly enhance the interactivity and user experience of your app. AppCraft provides a range of animation actions and effects that allow you to add dynamic and engaging animations to your app.

Transition Animations

Transition animations are commonly used to provide smooth transitions between different screens or elements within your app.

AppCraft allows you to define transition animations that are triggered when a user navigates between screens or interacts with specific elements. These animations can include fades, slides, rotations, and more.

Interactive Animations

Interactive animations are animations that respond to user input or interactions. For example, you can create animations that are triggered when a user taps on a button or swipes on a screen. AppCraft provides actions and functions that allow you to define interactive animations and control their behavior based on user input.

Feedback Animations

Feedback animations are used to provide visual feedback to the user based on their input or actions. For example, you can create animations that highlight a selected item or provide visual cues when a user successfully completes a task. AppCraft allows you to define feedback animations that enhance the user experience and make your app more engaging.

In this section, we have explored various techniques for implementing user input and interactivity in your AppCraft app. By effectively capturing user input, validating it, and responding to it, you can create a more engaging and interactive app experience for your users. Additionally, by incorporating animations, you can further enhance the interactivity and user experience of your app.

Integrating APIs and Services

Integrating APIs (Application Programming Interfaces) and services into your app can greatly enhance its functionality and provide users with a seamless experience. APIs allow your app to communicate and interact with external systems, such as social media platforms, payment gateways, mapping services, and more. By leveraging APIs and services, you can access a wide range of features and data that can take your app to the next level.

Understanding APIs

Before diving into the process of integrating APIs into your app, it's important to understand what APIs are and how they work. An API acts as a bridge between your app and external systems, allowing them to exchange data and perform actions. APIs provide a set of rules and protocols that define how different software components should interact with each other.

APIs come in different forms, such as RESTful APIs, SOAP APIs, and GraphQL APIs. RESTful APIs are the most common type and are widely used in app development. They use HTTP methods like GET, POST, PUT, and DELETE to perform operations on resources exposed by the API.

When integrating an API into your app, you need to obtain an API key or access token from the service provider. This key acts as a unique identifier for your app and allows the API to authenticate and authorize your requests. It's important to keep your API keys secure and avoid exposing them in your app's source code.

Choosing the Right APIs and Services

When selecting APIs and services to integrate into your app, it's crucial to consider your app's requirements and target audience. Here are some factors to consider when choosing APIs and services:

1. Functionality: Identify the specific features and functionalities you want to add to your app. For example, if you're building a social media app, you might want to integrate APIs for user authentication, posting updates, and retrieving user profiles.

2. Reliability and Performance: Ensure that the APIs and services you choose are reliable and have a good track record of uptime and performance. Slow or unreliable APIs can negatively impact your app's user experience.

3. Documentation and Support: Look for APIs and services that provide comprehensive documentation and developer support. Good documentation makes it easier for you to understand how to integrate the API into your app, while developer support can help you troubleshoot any issues that

may arise.

4. Pricing: Consider the pricing models of the APIs and services you're considering. Some APIs offer free tiers with limited usage, while others require a paid subscription. Make sure to evaluate the cost implications and choose an option that aligns with your budget.

5. Security: Ensure that the APIs and services you integrate into your app have proper security measures in place. This is especially important if your app deals with sensitive user data or financial transactions.

Integrating APIs into Your App

Once you have chosen the APIs and services you want to integrate into your app, the next step is to implement the integration. The process may vary depending on the app development platform or framework you are using, but the general steps are as follows:

1. Obtain API Credentials: Sign up for an account with the service provider and obtain the necessary API credentials, such as an API key or access token.

2. Read the Documentation: Familiarize yourself with the API documentation provided by the service provider. The documentation will guide you on how to make requests, handle responses, and implement the desired functionality.

3. Set Up API Requests: Use the programming language or framework of your choice to make API requests. This typically involves constructing HTTP requests with the appropriate headers, parameters, and payload.

4. Handle API Responses: Once you receive a response from the API, parse and process the data according to your app's requirements. This may involve extracting specific information, displaying it to the user, or storing it in your app's database.

5. Error Handling: Implement error handling mechanisms to handle cases where API requests fail or return errors. This ensures that your app gracefully handles any issues that may arise during API integration.

6. Test and Debug: Thoroughly test your app's integration with the API to ensure that it functions as expected. Use debugging tools and techniques to identify and fix any issues that may arise during the integration process.

7. Monitor and Maintain: Regularly monitor the API integration in your app to ensure that it continues to function properly. Keep an eye on any updates or changes made by the service provider that may require adjustments in your app's code.

Common API Integration Challenges

Integrating APIs into your app can sometimes present challenges that you need to overcome. Here are some common challenges and tips for addressing them:

1. Authentication and Authorization: Ensure that you correctly implement the authentication and authorization mechanisms required by the API. This may involve securely storing and managing API keys or access tokens.

2. Rate Limiting: Some APIs impose rate limits to prevent abuse and ensure fair usage. Make sure to understand and adhere to the rate limits imposed by the API to avoid disruptions in your app's functionality.

3. Handling Errors and Exceptions: APIs may return errors or exceptions in certain scenarios. Implement robust error handling mechanisms to gracefully handle these situations and provide meaningful feedback to the user.

4. Versioning and Deprecation: APIs can undergo changes, including version updates and deprecations. Stay updated with the service provider's documentation and announcements to ensure that your app remains compatible

with the latest API versions.

5. Performance Optimization: Intensive API usage can impact your app's performance. Implement caching mechanisms, optimize API requests, and consider asynchronous processing to minimize any performance bottlenecks.

By effectively integrating APIs and services into your app, you can unlock a world of possibilities and provide users with a rich and dynamic experience. Take the time to research and choose the right APIs and services for your app, and follow best practices for integration to ensure a smooth and seamless user experience.

Implementing App Notifications

App notifications play a crucial role in engaging and retaining users. They provide a way to communicate important information, updates, and reminders to users even when they are not actively using the app. Implementing app notifications effectively can significantly enhance the user experience and increase user engagement with your app. In this section, we will explore the process of implementing app notifications using AppCraft.

Understanding App Notifications

Before we dive into the implementation details, let's first understand what app notifications are and how they work. App notifications are messages that are sent from your app to the user's device, appearing as alerts, banners, or badges. These notifications can be triggered by various events, such as new messages, updates, reminders, or any other relevant information.

App notifications can be categorized into two types: local notifications and remote notifications. Local notifications are generated and scheduled by the app itself, while remote notifications are sent from a remote server to the user's device. Both types of notifications can be implemented in AppCraft.

Implementing Local Notifications

Local notifications are a great way to keep users informed about events or updates within your app. They can be used to remind users about upcoming tasks, notify them about new content, or simply provide them with relevant information. Implementing local notifications in AppCraft is a straightforward process.

To implement local notifications in AppCraft, you will need to use the "Notification" component. This component allows you to configure the content, appearance, and behavior of the notification. You can set the title, message, icon, and other properties of the notification to customize its appearance.

To trigger a local notification, you can use an event or action within your app. For example, you can schedule a notification to be triggered at a specific time or when a certain condition is met. You can also set the notification to repeat at regular intervals if needed.

Once the notification is triggered, it will be displayed on the user's device according to the device's notification settings. The user can then interact with the notification by tapping on it, which can open the app or perform a specific action within the app.

Implementing Remote Notifications

Remote notifications, also known as push notifications, are a powerful way to engage users and provide real-time updates. Unlike local notifications, remote notifications are sent from a remote server to the user's device. Implementing remote notifications in AppCraft requires some additional setup and configuration.

To implement remote notifications in AppCraft, you will need to integrate with a push notification service provider, such as Firebase Cloud Messaging (FCM) or Apple Push Notification Service (APNS). These services provide the infrastructure and APIs to send push notifications to devices.

The process of implementing remote notifications involves the following steps:

1. Set up an account with a push notification service provider and obtain the necessary credentials and API keys.

2. Configure your app in AppCraft to enable push notifications and provide the required credentials.
3. Implement the necessary code in your app to handle push notifications and register the device with the push notification service.
4. Use the push notification service's API to send notifications from your server to the user's device.

Once the remote notifications are set up and configured, you can send notifications to your users based on specific events or triggers. These notifications can contain custom content, such as text, images, or even interactive buttons.

Best Practices for App Notifications

To ensure that your app notifications are effective and well-received by users, it is important to follow some best practices. Here are some tips to consider when implementing app notifications in AppCraft:

1. Provide value: Make sure that your notifications provide relevant and valuable information to the users. Avoid sending unnecessary or spammy notifications that can annoy users.

2. Personalize notifications: Use user data and preferences to personalize the content of your notifications. Personalized notifications are more likely to be engaging and useful to the users.

3. Optimize timing: Consider the timing of your notifications to maximize their impact. Avoid sending notifications at inconvenient times, such as late at night or during important meetings.

4. Allow user control: Give users the ability to control the frequency and types of notifications they receive. Provide options for users to customize their notification settings within the app.

5. Test and iterate: Continuously test and iterate on your notification strategy to optimize its effectiveness. Monitor

user engagement and feedback to make improvements and adjustments as needed.

By following these best practices, you can ensure that your app notifications are well-received and contribute to a positive user experience. Implementing app notifications in your app can greatly enhance user engagement and provide valuable updates and information to your users. In this section, we explored the process of implementing both local and remote notifications using AppCraft. We discussed the different types of notifications, the components and configurations required, and best practices to follow. By effectively implementing app notifications, you can keep your users informed, engaged, and coming back to your app for more.

6.Publishing Your App

Preparing Your App for Publishing

Once you have completed the development and testing of your app, it's time to prepare it for publishing. This process involves a series of steps to ensure that your app is ready to be released to the public and made available for download on various app stores. In this section, we will discuss the key considerations and tasks involved in preparing your app for publishing.

App Store Guidelines and Requirements

Before you begin the publishing process, it is crucial to familiarize yourself with the guidelines and requirements of the app stores where you plan to distribute your app. Each app store has its own set of rules and regulations that govern the submission and review process. These guidelines cover various aspects such as app content, design, functionality, and security.

Some common guidelines include:

- App content: Ensure that your app does not contain any offensive, illegal, or inappropriate content. It should also comply with copyright and intellectual property laws.

- Design and user experience: Your app should have a visually appealing and intuitive user interface. It should follow the design principles and guidelines provided by the app store.

- Functionality: Your app should function as intended and should not have any bugs or crashes. It should provide a seamless user experience and should not violate any platform-specific functionality restrictions.

- Security and privacy: Your app should handle user data securely and should not collect or transmit any sensitive information without proper consent. It should also comply with privacy laws and regulations.

By understanding and adhering to these guidelines, you can ensure that your app meets the requirements of the app stores and increases the chances of a successful submission.

App Store Developer Accounts

To publish your app on most app stores, you will need to create a developer account. This account allows you to submit and manage your apps, track their performance, and receive payments for any sales or in-app purchases.

The process of creating a developer account varies depending on the app store. Some app stores require a one-time registration fee, while others may charge an annual fee. Additionally, you may need to provide certain information such as your contact details, tax information, and banking details for payment processing.

It is important to note that the account creation process may take some time, as the app store may need to verify your information before granting you access to their developer portal. Therefore, it is advisable to create your developer account well in advance to avoid any delays in the publishing process.

App Store Optimization (ASO)

App Store Optimization (ASO) is the process of optimizing your app's listing on the app store to improve its visibility and discoverability. ASO involves various techniques and strategies to increase your app's chances of appearing in search results and attracting potential users.

Some key aspects of ASO include:

- App title and description: Choose a descriptive and catchy title for your app that accurately represents its purpose. Write a compelling and informative app description that highlights its key features and benefits.

- Keywords: Research and identify relevant keywords that users are likely to search for when looking for apps similar to yours. Incorporate these keywords strategically in your app's title, description, and other metadata.

- App icon and screenshots: Design an eye-catching app icon that reflects your app's branding and purpose. Include high-quality screenshots that showcase the app's user interface and key features.

- Ratings and reviews: Encourage users to rate and review your app on the app store. Positive ratings and reviews can significantly impact your app's visibility and credibility.

- Localization: Consider localizing your app's listing to target specific regions and languages. This can help you reach a wider audience and improve user engagement.

By implementing effective ASO strategies, you can increase the visibility of your app on the app store and attract more potential users.

App Store Assets and Materials

Before submitting your app to the app store, you will need to gather and prepare various assets and materials required for the submission process. These assets include:

- App icon: Create a high-resolution app icon that meets the specifications provided by the app store. The app icon should be visually appealing and represent your app's branding.

- Screenshots and videos: Capture screenshots and record videos that showcase the key features and functionality of your app. These assets help users understand what your app offers and can influence their decision to download it.

- App description and metadata: Write a compelling app description that accurately represents your app's features and benefits. Prepare other metadata such as keywords, categories, and pricing information as required by the app store.

- Privacy policy: If your app collects any user data, you may need to provide a privacy policy that outlines how the data is collected, used, and protected. This is a crucial requirement to ensure compliance with privacy laws and regulations.

Ensure that all the assets and materials are prepared and organized according to the specifications provided by the app store. This will help streamline the submission process and avoid any delays or rejections.

App Store Submission and Review Process

Once you have prepared all the necessary assets and materials, you can proceed with submitting your app to the app store. The submission process typically involves the following steps:

1. Fill out the app submission form: Provide all the required information about your app, including its title, description, keywords, categories, and pricing details. Upload the app icon, screenshots, and other assets as specified by the app

store.

2. Review and validate the submission: Double-check all the information and assets to ensure they meet the app store's guidelines and requirements. Validate the submission to identify any potential issues or errors that may cause the app to be rejected.

3. Submit the app for review: Once you are satisfied with the submission, submit your app for review by the app store's team. The review process may take several days or even weeks, depending on the app store and the volume of submissions.

4. Address any feedback or issues: If the app store's review team identifies any issues or requests changes, make the necessary adjustments and resubmit your app for review. It is important to promptly address any feedback to avoid delays in the publishing process.

5. App approval and release: Once your app passes the review process, it will be approved for release on the app store. The app store will assign a release date, and your app will become available for download to users.

It is important to note that the review process is designed to ensure the quality and security of apps on the app store. Therefore, it is crucial to follow the guidelines and requirements provided by the app store to increase the chances of a successful review and approval.

Beta Testing and User Feedback

Before submitting your app for review, it is highly recommended to conduct beta testing and gather user feedback. Beta testing allows you to identify and fix any issues or bugs in your app before it is released to the public.

You can invite a group of beta testers to install and use your app, and encourage them to provide feedback on their experience. This feedback can help you identify usability issues, performance problems, and any other areas that need improvement.

By addressing the feedback and making necessary improvements, you can ensure that your app is of high quality and provides a positive user experience. This can significantly increase the chances of positive reviews and ratings, which in turn can boost your app's visibility and downloads on the app store.

In conclusion, preparing your app for publishing involves understanding the app store guidelines, creating a developer account, optimizing your app's listing, gathering and preparing the required assets, and going through the submission and review process. By following these steps and best practices, you can increase the chances of a successful app launch and maximize its potential for success in the app stores.

Generating App Builds for Different Platforms

Once you have completed the development and testing of your app, the next step is to generate app builds for different platforms. This process involves creating executable files that can be installed and run on specific operating systems such as iOS, Android, or Windows. In this section, we will explore the steps and considerations involved in generating app builds for different platforms.

Understanding Platform-Specific Requirements

Before generating app builds, it is crucial to understand the specific requirements and guidelines for each platform. Different platforms have their own set of rules and standards that need to be followed to ensure compatibility and optimal performance. Here are some key considerations for popular platforms:

iOS

To generate an app build for iOS, you need to have access to a Mac computer running macOS. Apple requires developers to use Xcode, their official integrated development environment (IDE), to build and submit iOS apps. Xcode provides tools for code editing, debugging, and app signing. Additionally, you need to enroll in the Apple Developer Program and obtain a valid provisioning profile and distribution certificate to sign your app.

Android

For Android app builds, you can use a Windows, macOS, or Linux computer. Android apps are typically built using Android Studio, the official IDE for Android development. Android Studio provides a rich set of tools for designing, coding, and testing Android apps. You will also need to create a signing key and configure the necessary build settings to generate a signed APK (Android Package) file for distribution.

Windows

To generate app builds for Windows, you can use a Windows computer. Windows apps can be built using Visual Studio, Microsoft's official IDE for Windows development. Visual Studio offers a wide range of tools and templates for building Windows apps, including Universal Windows Platform (UWP) apps that can run on multiple Windows devices. You will need to configure the build settings and sign the app using a valid certificate.

Building for iOS

To generate an app build for iOS, follow these steps:

1. Open Xcode on your Mac computer.
2. Select your app project from the project navigator.
3. Choose the target device (e.g., iPhone or iPad) and the desired build configuration (e.g., Debug or Release).
4. Configure the build settings, including the app display name, bundle identifier, and version number.
5. Select a valid provisioning profile and distribution certificate for code signing.
6. Build the app by clicking the "Build" button or using the keyboard shortcut (Cmd+B).
7. Once the build process is complete, Xcode will generate an app build file with the .ipa extension.

8. You can then distribute the app build for testing or submit it to the App Store for review and distribution.

Building for Android

To generate an app build for Android, follow these steps:

1. Open Android Studio on your computer.
2. Open your app project or create a new one.
3. Configure the build settings, including the app display name, package name, and version number, in the app's build.gradle file.
4. Create a signing key by going to "Build" > "Generate Signed Bundle/APK" and following the prompts. This will generate a keystore file that contains the signing information.
5. Build the app by clicking the "Build" button or using the keyboard shortcut (Ctrl+F9).
6. Once the build process is complete, Android Studio will generate an app build file with the .apk extension.
7. You can then distribute the app build for testing or upload it to the Google Play Store for review and distribution.

Building for Windows

To generate an app build for Windows, follow these steps:

1. Open Visual Studio on your Windows computer.
2. Open your app project or create a new one.
3. Configure the build settings, including the app display name, package name, and version number, in the app's manifest file.
4. Select the target device family and minimum version of Windows required for your app.
5. Build the app by clicking the "Build" button or using the keyboard shortcut (Ctrl+Shift+B).
6. Once the build process is complete, Visual Studio will generate an app build file with the .appx or .msix extension.
7. You can then distribute the app build for testing or submit it to the Microsoft Store for review and distribution.

Cross-Platform App Development

If you want to target multiple platforms with a single codebase, you can consider using cross-platform app development frameworks such as React Native, Flutter, or Xamarin. These frameworks allow you to write code once and generate app builds for multiple platforms. However, it is important to note that there may still be platform-specific considerations and adjustments required when using cross-platform frameworks.

Testing App Builds

Before distributing your app builds, it is crucial to thoroughly test them on the target platforms and devices. This ensures that your app functions correctly and provides a seamless user experience. Test your app builds on different devices, screen sizes, and operating system versions to identify and fix any compatibility issues or bugs.

Distributing App Builds

Once you have generated and tested your app builds, you can distribute them for testing or submit them to the respective app stores for review and distribution. Follow the guidelines and procedures provided by each platform to ensure a smooth submission process. It is important to comply with the platform-specific requirements, including app metadata, screenshots, and privacy policies.

In conclusion, generating app builds for different platforms involves understanding the specific requirements and guidelines for each platform, configuring the build settings, and using the appropriate tools and IDEs. Thorough testing and adherence to platform-specific guidelines are essential to ensure a successful app submission and distribution process.

Testing and Debugging Your App

Once you have designed and implemented the functionality of your app, it is crucial to thoroughly test and debug it before releasing it to the public. Testing and debugging are essential steps in the app development process to ensure that your app functions as intended and provides a seamless user experience. In this section, we will explore various testing and debugging techniques that you can use to identify and fix any issues or bugs in your app.

Testing Your App

Testing your app involves checking its functionality, performance, and usability to ensure that it meets the requirements and expectations of your users. There are several types of testing that you can perform on your app, including:

Functional Testing

Functional testing focuses on verifying that each feature and functionality of your app works correctly. It involves testing individual components, such as buttons, forms, and navigation, to ensure that they perform the intended actions. You can manually test your app by interacting with each element and verifying its behavior. Additionally, you can automate functional testing using testing frameworks and tools to simulate user interactions and validate the expected outcomes.

Usability Testing

Usability testing evaluates how easy and intuitive it is for users to navigate and interact with your app. It involves observing users as they perform specific tasks and collecting feedback on their experience. Usability testing can help you identify any usability issues, such as confusing navigation, unclear instructions, or difficult-to-use features. You can conduct usability testing by recruiting a group of target users and providing them with specific tasks to complete while observing their interactions and collecting their feedback.

Performance Testing

Performance testing assesses how well your app performs under different conditions, such as high user loads or limited network connectivity. It involves measuring response times, resource usage, and scalability to ensure that your app can handle the expected user traffic. Performance testing can help you identify any bottlenecks or performance issues that may affect the user experience. You can use performance testing tools to simulate various scenarios and measure the performance metrics of your app.

Compatibility Testing

Compatibility testing ensures that your app works correctly on different devices, operating systems, and screen sizes. It involves testing your app on a variety of devices, including smartphones, tablets, and different versions of operating systems, to ensure that it functions as intended. Compatibility testing can help you identify any device-specific issues or inconsistencies in the user interface. You can use emulators, simulators, or physical devices to perform compatibility testing.

Debugging Your App

Debugging is the process of identifying and fixing issues or bugs in your app's code. It involves analyzing the app's behavior, identifying the root cause of the problem, and implementing the necessary fixes. Here are some techniques and tools that can help you debug your app effectively:

Logging

Logging is a technique that allows you to record and analyze the execution flow and behavior of your app. By adding log statements at critical points in your code, you can track the values of variables, method calls, and error messages. Logging can help you identify the sequence of events leading to a bug and provide valuable insights into the app's behavior. You can use logging frameworks or built-in logging functions provided by your app building software to implement logging in your app.

Debugging Tools

Most app building software provides built-in debugging tools that can help you identify and fix issues in your app. These tools allow you to set breakpoints, step through your code, inspect variables, and analyze the call stack. By using the debugging tools provided by your app building software, you can pinpoint the exact location and cause of a bug and make the necessary code changes to fix it.

Error Handling

Implementing proper error handling in your app can help you identify and handle exceptions and errors gracefully. By catching and logging errors, you can gather information about the cause of the error and display meaningful error messages to the user. Error handling can prevent your app from crashing and provide a better user experience. Make sure to handle both expected and unexpected errors in your app's code.

Code Review

Performing code reviews with your team or peers can help identify potential issues or bugs in your app's code. By reviewing each other's code, you can spot logical errors, code inconsistencies, or inefficient code. Code reviews can also help ensure that your app follows best practices and coding standards. Consider using code review tools or platforms to facilitate the code review process and provide feedback to your team members.

Beta Testing

Beta testing involves releasing a pre-release version of your app to a limited group of users to gather feedback and identify any remaining issues. Beta testing allows you to test your app in a real-world environment and collect valuable insights from actual users. You can use beta testing platforms or distribute the beta version of your app to a selected group of users. Encourage beta testers to provide feedback, report bugs, and suggest improvements to help you refine your app before its official release.

Continuous Testing and Monitoring

Testing and debugging should not be limited to the development phase of your app. It is essential to establish a continuous testing and monitoring process to ensure that your app remains stable and performs well after its release. Continuous testing involves automating the testing process and running tests regularly to catch any regressions or issues introduced by new code changes. Continuous monitoring involves monitoring the performance and usage of your app in real-time to identify any anomalies or performance degradation.

By implementing continuous testing and monitoring, you can proactively identify and fix any issues that may arise in your app, ensuring a smooth user experience and maintaining the quality of your app over time.

In the next section, we will explore the process of submitting your app to app stores and the necessary steps to prepare your app for publishing.

Submitting Your App to App Stores

Once you have completed the development and testing of your app, the next step is to submit it to app stores for distribution. App stores are platforms where users can discover, download, and install apps on their devices. The two most popular app stores are the Apple App Store for iOS devices and the Google Play Store for Android devices. In this section, we will explore the process of submitting your app to these app stores and the guidelines you need to follow.

Apple App Store Submission Process

Submitting your app to the Apple App Store involves several steps. Here is an overview of the process:

1. **Create an Apple Developer Account**: Before you can submit your app to the App Store, you need to create an Apple Developer account. This account allows you to access the necessary tools and resources for app development and distribution.

2. **Prepare Your App for Submission**: Before submitting your app, make sure it meets all the requirements set by Apple. This includes ensuring that your app follows the App Store Review Guidelines, has a unique bundle identifier, and includes all the necessary metadata such as app name, description, screenshots, and app icon.

3. **Generate an App Store Distribution Certificate**: To distribute your app on the App Store, you need to create an App Store Distribution Certificate. This certificate is used to

sign your app and verify its authenticity.

4. **Create an App Store Listing**: The next step is to create a compelling app store listing. This includes writing an engaging app description, selecting relevant keywords, and uploading high-quality screenshots and app preview videos. You also need to provide information about the app's privacy policy and any in-app purchases.

5. **Submit Your App for Review**: Once you have prepared your app and created the app store listing, you can submit your app for review. Apple's App Review team will evaluate your app to ensure it meets the App Store Review Guidelines. The review process typically takes a few days, but it can vary depending on the complexity of your app.

6. **App Store Approval and Release**: If your app passes the review process, it will be approved for release on the App Store. You can then choose the release date and pricing options for your app. Once your app is live on the App Store, users can discover and download it on their iOS devices.

Google Play Store Submission Process

Submitting your app to the Google Play Store follows a similar process. Here are the steps involved:

1. **Create a Google Play Developer Account**: To submit your app to the Google Play Store, you need to create a Google Play Developer account. This account gives you access to the necessary tools and resources for app development and distribution.

2. **Prepare Your App for Submission**: Before submitting your app, ensure that it meets all the requirements set by Google. This includes following the Google Play Developer Program Policies, providing accurate app information, and including all the necessary assets such as app name, description, screenshots, and app icon.

3. **Generate a Release APK**: To distribute your app on the Google Play Store, you need to generate a release APK (Android Package). This APK is signed with a release key, which verifies the authenticity of your app.

4. **Create a Google Play Store Listing**: Similar to the Apple App Store, you need to create an appealing Google Play Store listing for your app. This includes writing a compelling app description, selecting relevant categories and tags, and uploading high-quality screenshots and promotional graphics.

5. **Submit Your App for Review**: Once you have prepared your app and created the store listing, you can submit your app for review. Google's review process ensures that your app complies with the Google Play Developer Program Policies. The review process usually takes a few hours to a few days.

6. **Google Play Store Approval and Release**: If your app passes the review process, it will be approved for release on the Google Play Store. You can then choose the release date and pricing options for your app. Once your app is live on the Google Play Store, users can discover and download it on their Android devices.

Additional Considerations

When submitting your app to app stores, there are a few additional considerations to keep in mind:

1. **App Store Guidelines**: Both Apple and Google have specific guidelines that you need to follow when submitting your app. These guidelines cover various aspects such as content, functionality, user experience, and privacy. It is essential to review and adhere to these guidelines to ensure your app is accepted.

2. **App Store Fees**: Both Apple and Google charge fees for app submissions and distribution. These fees may vary depending on factors such as the type of app, the pricing

model, and the region. Make sure to familiarize yourself with the fee structure of each app store before submitting your app.

3. **Localization**: Consider localizing your app to reach a broader audience. This involves translating your app's content and adapting it to different languages and cultures. Localization can significantly improve the discoverability and user experience of your app.

4. **App Store Optimization**: To increase the visibility of your app in app stores, you can optimize your app store listing using App Store Optimization (ASO) techniques. ASO involves optimizing your app's metadata, keywords, and visuals to improve its ranking in search results and increase downloads.

5. **App Store Analytics**: Once your app is live on app stores, it is crucial to track its performance using app store analytics. These analytics provide valuable insights into user behavior, app downloads, and user reviews. Analyzing this data can help you make informed decisions to improve your app's performance and user satisfaction.

Submitting your app to app stores is an exciting milestone in your app building journey. It allows you to share your app with a wide audience and potentially generate revenue. By following the submission guidelines and considering the additional factors mentioned above, you can increase the chances of your app being accepted and achieving success in the app stores.

7. App Marketing and Monetization

Creating an App Marketing Strategy

Once you have built your app using AppCraft, the next step is to create an effective app marketing strategy. A well-planned marketing strategy is crucial for the success of your app, as it helps you reach your target audience, increase app visibility, and drive downloads and user engagement. In this section, we will explore the key steps involved in creating an app marketing strategy.

Define Your Target Audience

Before you start promoting your app, it is important to clearly define your target audience. Understanding who your app is designed for will help you tailor your marketing efforts and reach the right people. Consider factors such as age, gender, location, interests, and behavior patterns. Conduct market research and analyze your competitors to identify gaps and opportunities in the market.

Set Clear Goals

To create an effective app marketing strategy, you need to set clear goals. What do you want to achieve with your app? Do you want to increase downloads, drive user engagement, generate revenue, or all of the above? Setting specific, measurable, achievable, relevant, and time-bound (SMART) goals will help you stay focused and track your progress.

Research App Store Optimization (ASO)

App Store Optimization (ASO) is the process of optimizing your app's visibility in the app stores. It involves optimizing your app's title, keywords, description, and screenshots to improve its ranking in search results. Research popular keywords related to your app and incorporate them strategically in your app's metadata. Analyze your competitors' app store listings to gain insights and identify areas for improvement.

Create Compelling App Store Listing

Your app store listing is the first impression users have of your app. It should be visually appealing, informative, and persuasive. Use high-quality screenshots and videos to showcase your app's features and benefits. Write a compelling app description that highlights its unique selling points and appeals to your target audience. Encourage users to leave positive reviews and ratings to improve your app's credibility.

Leverage Social Media

Social media platforms are powerful tools for promoting your app and engaging with your target audience. Create social media accounts for your app on platforms such as Facebook, Twitter, Instagram, and LinkedIn. Share engaging content related to your app, such as tutorials, tips, and updates. Run targeted ads to reach a wider audience and drive app downloads. Encourage users to share their experiences with your app on social media.

Implement Content Marketing

Content marketing involves creating and sharing valuable content to attract and engage your target audience. Create a blog or website for your app and regularly publish informative and relevant articles. Optimize your content for search engines to improve its visibility. Offer valuable resources, such as e-books, whitepapers, or video tutorials, to establish yourself as an authority in your app's niche.

Engage with Influencers

Influencer marketing is a popular strategy for promoting apps. Identify influencers in your app's niche who have a large and engaged following. Reach out to them and offer them a free download or access to premium features in exchange for a review or promotion. Influencers can help you reach a wider audience and build credibility for your app.

Run App Install Campaigns

Running app install campaigns is an effective way to drive app downloads. Platforms such as Google Ads and Facebook Ads allow you to target specific demographics and interests. Create compelling ad creatives that highlight your app's unique features and benefits. Monitor and optimize your campaigns regularly to maximize your return on investment (ROI).

Implement App Analytics

App analytics provide valuable insights into user behavior and app performance. Implement a robust analytics tool, such as Google Analytics or Firebase Analytics, to track key metrics such as app downloads, user engagement, retention, and in-app purchases. Analyze the data to identify areas for improvement and make data-driven decisions to optimize your app marketing strategy.

Monitor and Iterate

App marketing is an ongoing process. Monitor the performance of your app marketing efforts and iterate based on the results. Continuously test different marketing channels, messaging, and strategies to find what works best for your app. Stay updated with the latest trends and changes in the app marketing landscape to stay ahead of the competition.

By following these steps and continuously refining your app marketing strategy, you can increase the visibility and success of your app. Remember that app marketing requires time, effort, and experimentation. Stay persistent and adapt your strategy based on user feedback and market trends. Good luck with your app marketing journey!

Optimizing Your App Store Listing

Once you have developed your app using AppCraft, the next step is to optimize your app store listing. This is a crucial aspect of app marketing as it directly impacts the visibility and discoverability of your app. A well-optimized app store listing can significantly increase the number of downloads and user engagement. In this section, we will explore the key strategies and best practices for optimizing your app store listing.

App Title and Icon

The first impression of your app is formed by its title and icon. It is essential to choose a catchy and descriptive app title that reflects the purpose and functionality of your app. The title should be concise, memorable, and easy to understand. Avoid using generic or misleading titles that may confuse potential users.

Equally important is the app icon. The icon should be visually appealing, unique, and representative of your app's brand. It should stand out among other app icons and convey the essence of your app. Make sure the icon is optimized for different screen sizes and resolutions to ensure a consistent and high-quality appearance.

App Description

The app description plays a crucial role in convincing users to download your app. It should provide a clear and concise overview of your app's features, benefits, and unique selling points. Use persuasive language to highlight the value proposition of your app and explain how it solves a specific problem or meets a particular need.

To make your app description more engaging, consider using bullet points or short paragraphs to break down the information into easily digestible chunks. Use keywords strategically throughout the description to improve search visibility and attract relevant users. However, avoid keyword stuffing, as it can negatively impact the readability and credibility of your app description.

Screenshots and Videos

Visual assets such as screenshots and videos are powerful tools for showcasing your app's user interface and functionality. They provide potential users with a glimpse of what to expect from your app and can significantly influence their decision to download it.

When creating screenshots, focus on highlighting the most compelling features and user experience of your app. Use captions or annotations to provide context and explain the key functionalities. Ensure that the screenshots are of high quality, properly sized, and optimized for different devices.

Videos can be even more impactful in conveying the value of your app. Consider creating a short promotional video that demonstrates the key features and benefits of your app. Keep the video concise, engaging, and visually appealing. Add captions or voiceover to explain the app's functionalities and benefits clearly.

App Ratings and Reviews

Positive app ratings and reviews are essential for building trust and credibility among potential users. Encourage your existing users to leave reviews and ratings by implementing in-app prompts or reminders. Respond to user reviews promptly, addressing any concerns or issues raised. Engaging with your users and providing excellent customer support can lead to positive reviews and higher ratings.

To maintain a high rating, regularly update your app with bug fixes, performance improvements, and new features. Respond to user feedback and continuously strive to enhance the user experience. A high rating and positive reviews can significantly impact your app's visibility and conversion rate.

App Keywords

App store optimization (ASO) relies heavily on the strategic use of keywords. Keywords are the words or phrases that users enter in the app store search bar when looking for specific apps. By incorporating relevant keywords in your app's title, description, and metadata, you can improve its visibility in search results.

Research and identify the most relevant and high-traffic keywords for your app. Consider using tools like Google Keyword Planner or App Store Optimization tools to find popular keywords related to your app's category and functionality. Incorporate these keywords naturally throughout your app store listing to increase its chances of appearing in relevant search results.

Localization

Localization is the process of adapting your app to different languages and cultures. By localizing your app store listing, you can reach a broader audience and increase your app's visibility in different regions. Translate your app title, description, and keywords into the languages of your target markets.

When localizing your app store listing, consider cultural nuances and preferences. Adapt your screenshots, videos, and promotional materials to resonate with the target audience. Localizing your app can significantly improve its discoverability and appeal to users who prefer apps in their native language.

A/B Testing

A/B testing is a valuable technique for optimizing your app store listing. It involves creating multiple variations of your app store assets, such as titles, icons, screenshots, and descriptions, and testing them against each other to determine which version performs better.

By conducting A/B tests, you can gather data and insights on user preferences and behavior. Test different variations of your app store assets and analyze the performance metrics, such as conversion rate and download numbers. Use the results to refine and optimize your app store listing continuously.

App Store Optimization Tools

Several tools and platforms are available to help you optimize your app store listing effectively. These tools provide insights, analytics, and recommendations to improve your app's visibility and conversion rate. Some popular ASO tools include Sensor Tower, App Annie, Mobile Action, and App Radar.

Leverage these tools to conduct keyword research, track your app's performance, monitor competitors, and gain valuable insights into user behavior. Regularly analyze the data and make data-driven decisions to optimize your app store listing for maximum impact.

By implementing these strategies and best practices, you can optimize your app store listing and increase the visibility and discoverability of your app. Remember to continuously monitor and refine your app store assets based on user feedback and market trends. A well-optimized app store listing can significantly contribute to the success of your app and drive higher downloads and user engagement.

Implementing In-App Purchases and Ads

Once you have built your app and are ready to monetize it, implementing in-app purchases and ads can be a great way to generate revenue. In this section, we will explore how to integrate these features into your app using AppCraft.

Understanding In-App Purchases

In-app purchases allow users to buy additional content or features within your app. This can include items such as virtual goods, premium content, or subscriptions. Before implementing in-app purchases, it is important to understand the different types and how they work.

Consumable In-App Purchases

Consumable in-app purchases are items that can be purchased multiple times. For example, in a game, users can buy virtual currency or power-ups that can be used up and then repurchased. To implement consumable in-app purchases in AppCraft, you will need to set up a store and define the products available for purchase.

Non-Consumable In-App Purchases

Non-consumable in-app purchases are items that users can buy once and keep forever. For example, in an e-book reader app, users can purchase individual books that they can access anytime. To implement non-consumable in-app purchases in AppCraft, you will need to set up a store and define the products available for purchase.

Subscriptions

Subscriptions allow users to access content or features for a specific period of time. For example, in a music streaming app, users can subscribe to a monthly plan to access unlimited music. To implement subscriptions in AppCraft, you will need to set up a store and define the subscription options available.

Setting Up In-App Purchases in AppCraft

To implement in-app purchases in your AppCraft app, you will need to follow these steps:

1. Set up a developer account: Before you can enable in-app purchases, you will need to create a developer account with the respective app store (such as the Apple App Store or Google Play Store).

2. Configure in-app purchases: In AppCraft, navigate to the "In-App Purchases" section and configure the necessary settings. This includes specifying the product details, pricing, and availability.

3. Implement the purchase flow: In your app, you will need to add the necessary buttons or links to trigger the purchase flow. When a user initiates a purchase, you will need to handle the transaction and provide the purchased content or features.

4. Test the in-app purchases: Before releasing your app, it is crucial to thoroughly test the in-app purchase functionality. You can use test accounts provided by the app stores to simulate purchases and ensure everything is working correctly.

Implementing Ads in Your App

In addition to in-app purchases, integrating ads into your app can be another effective way to monetize it. AppCraft provides support for various ad networks, allowing you to display ads within your app and earn revenue based on user interactions.

Choosing an Ad Network

Before implementing ads, you will need to choose an ad network that best suits your app and target audience. Some popular ad networks include Google AdMob, Facebook Audience Network, and Unity Ads. Each network has its own requirements and integration process.

Configuring Ad Units

Once you have chosen an ad network, you will need to configure ad units within your AppCraft project. Ad units define the type and placement of ads within your app. This can include banner ads, interstitial ads, rewarded video ads, and more.

Implementing Ad Display

To display ads in your app, you will need to add the necessary components and code snippets provided by the ad network. AppCraft makes it easy to integrate ads by providing pre-built components and templates for popular ad networks. Simply drag and drop the components into your app's screens and configure them with your ad unit IDs.

Testing Ads

Before releasing your app, it is important to test the ad integration to ensure everything is working correctly. Most ad networks provide test ad IDs that you can use during the testing phase. This allows you to verify that ads are being displayed properly and that you are earning revenue from user interactions.

Monetization Strategies

Implementing in-app purchases and ads is just the beginning of your app monetization journey. To maximize your revenue, it is important to consider the following strategies:

Offer a Freemium Model

A freemium model allows users to download and use your app for free, but offers additional premium features or content through in-app purchases. This can entice users to upgrade to the premium version and generate revenue.

Implement Targeted Ads

By using ad networks that offer targeted advertising, you can display ads that are relevant to your users' interests. This increases the chances of users engaging with the ads and generating revenue for your app.

Analyze User Behavior

Use analytics tools to track user behavior within your app. This can help you understand which features or content are most popular and optimize your monetization strategy accordingly.

Continuously Update and Improve

Regularly update your app with new features, content, and bug fixes. This keeps users engaged and encourages them to make in-app purchases or interact with ads.

Implementing in-app purchases and ads can be a lucrative way to monetize your app. By understanding the different types of in-app purchases, setting up the necessary configurations in AppCraft, and choosing the right ad network, you can effectively generate revenue and maximize the success of your app. Remember to continuously analyze user behavior and update your app to keep it fresh and engaging.

Tracking and Analyzing App Performance

Tracking and analyzing app performance is a crucial aspect of app development. By monitoring and evaluating how your app performs, you can identify areas for improvement, optimize its performance, and provide a better user experience. In this section, we will explore various techniques and tools that can help you track and analyze the performance of your app.

Importance of App Performance Tracking

Tracking app performance allows you to gain insights into how your app is functioning in real-world scenarios. It helps you understand how users interact with your app, identify any bottlenecks or issues that may arise, and make data-driven decisions to enhance its performance. Here are some key reasons why tracking app performance is important:

1. User Experience Optimization

App performance directly impacts the user experience. By tracking performance metrics, such as app load time, response time, and overall responsiveness, you can identify areas where your app may be lagging or causing frustration for users. This information can guide you in optimizing your app to provide a smoother and more enjoyable user experience.

2. Bug Detection and Troubleshooting

Tracking app performance can help you identify and diagnose any bugs or issues that may arise. By monitoring performance metrics, you can pinpoint specific areas of your app that may be causing crashes, slow response times, or other performance-related problems. This allows you to quickly address these issues and provide a more stable and reliable app for your users.

3. Performance Optimization

Analyzing app performance data can provide valuable insights into areas where your app may be underperforming or consuming excessive resources. By identifying these bottlenecks, you can optimize your app's code, improve resource management, and enhance overall performance. This can lead to faster load times, smoother animations, and improved battery life for your users.

4. User Retention and Engagement

A poorly performing app can lead to user frustration and abandonment. By tracking app performance, you can ensure that your app meets the expectations of your users and provides a seamless experience. This can help increase user retention, engagement, and ultimately, the success of your app.

Key Performance Metrics to Track

To effectively track and analyze app performance, it is important to monitor key performance metrics. These metrics provide valuable insights into how your app is performing and can help you identify areas for improvement. Here are some essential performance metrics to consider tracking:

1. App Load Time

App load time refers to the time it takes for your app to launch and become fully functional. This metric is crucial as it directly impacts the user's first impression of your app. Monitoring app load time allows you to identify any bottlenecks or delays that may be affecting the user experience.

2. Response Time

Response time measures how quickly your app responds to user interactions, such as button clicks or screen transitions. A slow response time can lead to user frustration and a poor user experience. By tracking response time, you can identify areas where your app may be lagging and optimize its performance.

3. CPU and Memory Usage

Monitoring CPU and memory usage provides insights into how your app utilizes system resources. High CPU or memory usage can lead to app crashes, slow performance, and drain the device's battery. By tracking these metrics, you can identify resource-intensive areas of your app and optimize them to improve overall performance.

4. Network Performance

For apps that rely on network connectivity, monitoring network performance is crucial. This includes tracking metrics such as network latency, download and upload speeds, and error rates. By monitoring network performance, you can identify any issues that may be affecting the app's ability to communicate with servers or load data efficiently.

Tools for App Performance Tracking and Analysis

To effectively track and analyze app performance, there are various tools available that provide valuable insights and metrics. Here are some popular tools that can help you monitor and optimize your app's performance:

1. Crash Reporting Tools

Crash reporting tools, such as Firebase Crashlytics and Microsoft App Center, help you track and analyze app crashes. These tools provide detailed crash reports, including stack traces and device information, allowing you to quickly identify and fix any issues that may be causing crashes.

2. Analytics Platforms

Analytics platforms, such as Google Analytics and Flurry Analytics, offer comprehensive tracking and analysis of user behavior within your app. These tools provide insights into user engagement, retention, and conversion rates. By analyzing this data, you can make informed decisions to improve your app's performance and user experience.

3. Performance Monitoring Tools

Performance monitoring tools, such as New Relic and Dynatrace, provide real-time monitoring of your app's performance. These tools track metrics like app load time, response time, CPU and memory usage, and network performance. They offer detailed dashboards and alerts to help you identify and address performance issues promptly.

4. User Feedback and Review Analysis Tools

User feedback and review analysis tools, such as Appbot and Apptentive, allow you to gather and analyze user feedback and reviews from app stores and other sources. These tools help you understand user sentiment, identify common issues, and prioritize improvements to enhance app performance.

Implementing App Performance Tracking

To implement app performance tracking effectively, follow these steps:

1. Define Performance Goals

Start by defining specific performance goals for your app. Determine the key metrics you want to track and improve. This will help you focus your efforts and measure the success of your performance optimization initiatives.

2. Choose App Performance Tracking Tools

Select the appropriate tools based on your performance tracking needs. Consider factors such as ease of integration, compatibility with your app development platform, and the specific metrics and insights provided by each tool.

3. Instrument Your App

Integrate the chosen performance tracking tools into your app. This typically involves adding the necessary code snippets or SDKs provided by the tools to your app's codebase. Follow the documentation and guidelines provided by the tools to ensure proper implementation.

4. Set Up Performance Monitoring

Configure the performance monitoring tools to track the desired metrics. Define thresholds or alerts to notify you when performance issues occur. This will allow you to proactively address any performance-related problems.

5. Analyze Performance Data

Regularly analyze the performance data collected by the tracking tools. Look for patterns, trends, and areas of improvement. Use this data to make informed decisions and prioritize optimizations to enhance your app's performance.

6. Iterate and Optimize

Continuously iterate and optimize your app based on the insights gained from performance tracking. Implement improvements, measure their impact on performance metrics, and refine your app to provide the best possible user experience.

By effectively tracking and analyzing app performance, you can identify areas for improvement, optimize your app's performance, and provide a better user experience. Use the tools and techniques discussed in this section to monitor and enhance the performance of your app throughout its lifecycle.

8.Advanced AppCraft Techniques

Working with Custom Code

As you become more experienced in app development, you may find that the built-in features and components of your chosen app building software may not always meet your specific needs. In such cases, working with custom code can provide you with the flexibility and control to implement advanced features and functionalities in your app. This section will guide you through the process of working with custom code in AppCraft.

Understanding the Role of Custom Code

Custom code refers to the programming language-specific instructions that you can write to extend the functionality of your app beyond what is provided by the app building software. It allows you to implement complex algorithms, integrate with external libraries or APIs, and create custom user interfaces. By leveraging custom code, you can unlock a world of possibilities and create unique and powerful apps.

Choosing the Right Programming Language

When working with custom code, it is essential to choose the right programming language that aligns with your app's requirements and your familiarity with the language. AppCraft supports a wide range of programming languages, including JavaScript, Swift, Kotlin, and C#. Each language has its strengths and weaknesses, so it's important to consider factors such as performance, platform compatibility, and community support when making your decision.

Integrating Custom Code in AppCraft

AppCraft provides a seamless integration of custom code within your app building workflow. To get started, you need to create a new custom code file within your project. This file acts as a container for your custom code and allows you to organize and manage your code effectively.

Once you have created the custom code file, you can start writing your code using the chosen programming language. AppCraft provides a code editor with syntax highlighting and auto-completion features to assist you in writing clean and error-free code. You can also leverage the built-in debugging tools to identify and fix any issues in your custom code.

Accessing AppCraft APIs and Services

One of the significant advantages of working with custom code in AppCraft is the ability to access and utilize the extensive range of APIs and services provided by the platform. These APIs and services cover various functionalities such as accessing device sensors, interacting with the file system, handling network requests, and much more.

By leveraging these APIs and services, you can enhance your app's capabilities and provide a seamless user experience. For example, you can use the camera API to capture and process images, integrate with social media platforms to enable sharing functionality, or utilize location services to provide location-based features.

Implementing Advanced Features

Working with custom code opens up a world of possibilities for implementing advanced features in your app. Here are a few examples of what you can achieve:

Machine Learning and Artificial Intelligence

By integrating machine learning and artificial intelligence libraries into your app, you can create intelligent features such as image recognition, natural language processing, and predictive analytics.

These advanced capabilities can provide personalized experiences and automate complex tasks within your app.

Augmented Reality and Virtual Reality

With the help of custom code, you can integrate augmented reality (AR) and virtual reality (VR) functionalities into your app. This allows you to create immersive experiences, such as interactive 3D models, virtual tours, and gamified elements, that can revolutionize the way users interact with your app.

Offline Functionality

Custom code enables you to implement offline functionality in your app, allowing users to access and interact with content even when they are not connected to the internet. By caching data and utilizing local storage, you can ensure that your app remains functional and provides a seamless experience in offline mode.

Best Practices for Working with Custom Code

When working with custom code, it's important to follow best practices to ensure the stability, maintainability, and performance of your app. Here are some tips to keep in mind:

- **Modularity**: Break your code into smaller, reusable modules to improve code organization and maintainability.
- **Documentation**: Document your custom code thoroughly to make it easier for other developers to understand and collaborate on your project.
- **Error Handling**: Implement proper error handling mechanisms to gracefully handle exceptions and prevent crashes in your app.
- **Testing**: Test your custom code thoroughly to identify and fix any bugs or issues before deploying your app.
- **Version Control**: Utilize version control systems like Git to track changes in your custom code and collaborate with other developers effectively.

Working with custom code in AppCraft allows you to extend the functionality of your app and implement advanced features that are not available out-of-the-box. By choosing the right programming language, integrating with AppCraft APIs and services, and following best practices, you can unlock the full potential of your app and create a truly unique and powerful user experience.

Implementing Advanced App Features

Once you have mastered the basics of app building and have created a functional app, it's time to take your skills to the next level. In this section, we will explore advanced app features that can enhance the functionality and user experience of your app. These features will help you create more sophisticated and powerful apps that stand out in the crowded app market.

Implementing Push Notifications

Push notifications are a powerful tool for engaging with your app users and keeping them informed about important updates and events. With push notifications, you can send messages directly to your users' devices, even when they are not actively using your app. This allows you to deliver timely information, such as new content, promotions, or reminders, and keep your users engaged.

To implement push notifications in your app, you will need to integrate with a push notification service provider, such as Firebase Cloud Messaging (FCM) or Apple Push Notification Service (APNS). These services provide the infrastructure and APIs necessary to send push notifications to different platforms, such as iOS and Android.

Once you have integrated with a push notification service, you can use the provided APIs to send notifications to specific users or groups of users. You can customize the content and appearance of the notifications, including the title, message, and any accompanying media. Additionally, you can track the delivery and engagement of your notifications to measure their effectiveness.

Implementing In-App Purchases

Monetizing your app is an important aspect of app development, and one popular method is through in-app purchases. In-app purchases allow users to buy additional content, features, or virtual goods within your app. This can include items like premium subscriptions, extra levels in a game, or virtual currency.

To implement in-app purchases, you will need to integrate with the app stores' in-app purchase APIs, such as Apple's StoreKit or Google Play Billing. These APIs provide the necessary functionality to handle the purchase flow, including presenting the user with the available products, processing the payment, and delivering the purchased content.

When implementing in-app purchases, it's important to carefully design your purchase flow to provide a seamless and intuitive experience for your users. Clearly communicate the value of the purchase and ensure that the process is secure and reliable. Additionally, consider offering different pricing tiers or subscription options to cater to a wider range of users.

Implementing Social Media Integration

Social media integration allows users to connect and share content from your app with their social networks. This can help increase the visibility and reach of your app, as well as provide a more personalized and social experience for your users.

To implement social media integration, you will need to integrate with the social media platforms' APIs, such as Facebook Login or Twitter API. These APIs provide the necessary functionality to authenticate users, access their social profiles, and post content on their behalf.

When implementing social media integration, consider the privacy and security implications for your users. Clearly communicate what data will be shared and how it will be used. Additionally, provide options for users to control their privacy settings and choose what content they want to share.

Implementing Location-Based Services

Location-based services can add a new dimension to your app by leveraging the user's location to provide personalized and context-aware content. With location-based services, you can offer features such as geolocation tracking, nearby points of interest, or location-based recommendations.

To implement location-based services, you will need to integrate with location services APIs, such as Google Maps API or Core Location framework. These APIs provide the necessary functionality to access the user's location, perform geocoding and reverse geocoding, and display maps and routes.

When implementing location-based services, it's important to consider the privacy and permissions required. Clearly communicate to your users why you need their location data and how it will be used. Additionally, provide options for users to control their location sharing settings and offer a seamless and intuitive user experience.

Implementing Offline Support

Offline support is crucial for apps that rely on real-time data or need to function in areas with limited or no internet connectivity. By implementing offline support, you can ensure that your app remains functional and provides a seamless user experience even when the user is offline.

To implement offline support, you will need to design and implement a local data storage mechanism, such as a local database or caching system. This allows your app to store and retrieve data locally, without relying on a network connection. Additionally, you will need to handle data synchronization when the app comes back online to ensure that the local data is up to date.

When implementing offline support, consider the size and complexity of the data that needs to be stored locally. Optimize the storage and retrieval processes to minimize the impact on device resources. Additionally, provide clear feedback to the user when the app is offline and inform them about the limitations of offline functionality.

Implementing Advanced User Authentication and Security

User authentication and security are critical aspects of app development, especially for apps that handle sensitive user data or require user accounts. Implementing advanced user authentication and security measures can help protect your app and your users' data from unauthorized access and ensure a secure user experience.

To implement advanced user authentication and security, consider using secure authentication methods such as biometric authentication (e.g., fingerprint or face recognition) or two-factor authentication. Additionally, implement secure data storage and transmission practices, such as encrypting sensitive data and using secure communication protocols.

When implementing advanced user authentication and security, it's important to balance security with usability. Avoid overly complex authentication processes that may frustrate or confuse users. Additionally, regularly update and patch your app to address any security vulnerabilities that may arise. Implementing advanced app features can take your app to the next level and provide a more engaging and personalized experience for your users. Whether it's implementing push notifications, in-app purchases, social media integration, location-based services, offline support, or advanced user authentication and security, these features can help differentiate your app from the competition and attract and retain users. Remember to carefully consider the needs and preferences of your target audience when implementing these features and continuously iterate and improve based on user feedback and analytics.

Optimizing App Performance

When it comes to building apps, performance is a crucial aspect that can make or break the success of your application. Users expect apps to be fast, responsive, and efficient, and if your app falls short in any of these areas, it can lead to a poor user experience and negative reviews. In this section, we will explore various techniques and strategies to optimize the performance of your app built with AppCraft.

Understanding App Performance

Before diving into optimization techniques, it's important to understand what app performance entails. App performance refers to how well your app performs in terms of speed, responsiveness, and resource usage. There are several key factors that can impact app performance:

Loading Time

The loading time of your app is the time it takes for the app to launch and become usable. Users expect apps to load quickly, and a slow loading time can lead to frustration and abandonment. Optimizing the loading time involves minimizing the app's startup time and reducing any delays in displaying the initial content.

Responsiveness

App responsiveness refers to how quickly the app responds to user interactions. A responsive app provides smooth and seamless user experiences, with minimal delays or lag. To optimize responsiveness, you need to ensure that your app's UI elements and interactions are fast and fluid.

Memory Usage

Memory usage is an important aspect of app performance. Apps that consume excessive memory can slow down the device and lead to crashes or instability. Optimizing memory usage involves managing and releasing resources efficiently, such as freeing up memory when it's no longer needed.

Battery Consumption

App performance also includes the impact on device battery life. Apps that drain the battery quickly can frustrate users and lead to negative reviews. Optimizing battery consumption involves minimizing unnecessary background processes, reducing CPU usage, and optimizing network requests.

Performance Optimization Techniques

Now that we have a clear understanding of app performance, let's explore some techniques to optimize the performance of your AppCraft app:

Minimize Network Requests

Reducing the number of network requests can significantly improve app performance, especially in scenarios where the app relies heavily on fetching data from remote servers. Minimize unnecessary API calls, combine multiple requests into a single batch request, and implement caching mechanisms to reduce the need for repeated network requests.

Optimize Image Loading

Images can be a major contributor to slow app performance. Optimize image loading by using compressed image formats, resizing images to the appropriate dimensions, and lazy loading images to load them only when they are visible on the screen. Additionally, consider using image caching techniques to improve the loading speed of images.

Implement Efficient Data Handling

Efficiently handling data within your app can have a significant impact on performance. Avoid loading large datasets all at once and instead implement pagination or infinite scrolling to load data in smaller chunks. Use data structures and algorithms that are optimized for performance, such as using indexes for faster data retrieval.

Optimize UI Rendering

UI rendering can be a resource-intensive process, especially when dealing with complex UI elements or animations. Optimize UI rendering by minimizing the number of UI updates, using lightweight UI components, and leveraging hardware acceleration when available. Consider using techniques like virtualization or recycling to efficiently render large lists or grids.

Background Processing

Performing heavy computations or resource-intensive tasks in the background can help improve app performance. Offload tasks that don't require immediate user interaction to background threads or services. However, be mindful of the impact on battery consumption and ensure that background tasks are properly managed and optimized.

Memory Management

Efficient memory management is crucial for app performance. Avoid memory leaks by properly releasing resources when they are no longer needed. Use memory profiling tools to identify and fix any memory-related issues. Consider implementing techniques like object pooling or lazy loading to optimize memory usage.

Code Optimization

Optimizing your code can have a significant impact on app performance. Use efficient algorithms and data structures, avoid unnecessary computations or iterations, and minimize the use of global variables. Profile your code to identify performance bottlenecks and optimize those areas for better performance.

Testing and Monitoring Performance

Optimizing app performance is an ongoing process that requires continuous testing and monitoring. Here are some strategies to ensure your app performs well:

Performance Testing

Perform regular performance testing to identify any performance bottlenecks or issues. Use profiling tools to measure the app's loading time, responsiveness, memory usage, and battery consumption. Conduct tests on different devices and network conditions to ensure optimal performance across various scenarios.

Crash Reporting and Error Monitoring

Implement crash reporting and error monitoring tools to track any crashes or errors that occur in your app. Analyze crash reports and error logs to identify performance-related issues and fix them promptly. Regularly review and address user-reported performance problems to improve the overall app experience.

Analytics and User Feedback

Leverage analytics tools to gather insights into how users interact with your app. Monitor user feedback and reviews to identify any performance-related concerns. Use this feedback to prioritize and address performance issues that impact the user experience. Optimizing app performance is crucial for delivering a high-quality user experience. By understanding the key factors that impact performance and implementing the optimization techniques discussed in this section, you can ensure that your AppCraft app performs efficiently and meets the expectations of your users. Regular testing and monitoring will help you identify and address any performance issues, ensuring that your app remains fast, responsive, and reliable.

Implementing App Localization

App localization is the process of adapting your app to different languages and cultures, making it accessible and appealing to a global audience. By implementing app localization, you can reach a wider user base and increase user engagement. In this section, we will explore the importance of app localization, the steps involved in the localization process, and best practices for implementing localization in your AppCraft app.

Understanding the Importance of App Localization

In today's interconnected world, users expect apps to be available in their native language. By localizing your app, you can provide a personalized experience to users from different regions, which can significantly enhance user satisfaction and engagement. Here are a few reasons why app localization is crucial:

1. **Expanded Market Reach**: By localizing your app, you can tap into new markets and reach a larger audience. Users are more likely to download and use an app that is available in their native language.

2. **Improved User Experience**: Localization allows users to interact with your app in a language they are comfortable with, making it easier for them to navigate, understand instructions, and engage with your app's features.

3. **Increased User Engagement**: When users feel that an app is designed specifically for them, they are more likely to engage with it, spend more time using it, and even recommend it to others.

4. **Competitive Advantage**: App localization can give you a competitive edge by differentiating your app from others in the market. By providing a localized experience, you can attract users who prefer apps in their native language.

Steps in the Localization Process

Implementing app localization in your AppCraft app involves several steps. Let's walk through the process:

1. **Identify Target Languages**: Determine the languages you want to localize your app into. Consider your target audience and market research to identify the languages that will have the most impact.

2. **Prepare App Resources**: Extract all the text strings and resources from your app that need to be translated. This includes UI labels, button text, error messages, and any other text displayed to the user.

3. **Translate Text Strings**: Hire professional translators or use translation services to translate the extracted text strings into the target languages. Ensure that the translations are accurate and culturally appropriate.

4. **Implement Localization in AppCraft**: In AppCraft, you can implement localization by creating language-specific versions of your app's screens and components. Use the translated text strings to replace the original text in the localized versions.

5. **Test and Refine**: Thoroughly test the localized versions of your app to ensure that the translations are accurate and that the app functions correctly in different languages. Make any necessary adjustments or refinements based on user feedback or testing results.

6. **Update App Store Listings**: Update your app's metadata and descriptions in the app stores to reflect the availability of localized versions. This will help users discover your app in their preferred language.

Best Practices for App Localization

To ensure a successful app localization process, consider the following best practices:

1. **Cultural Sensitivity**: Take cultural differences into account when localizing your app. Avoid using images, symbols, or text that may be offensive or misunderstood in different cultures.

2. **Contextual Translation**: Provide context to translators to ensure accurate translations. Share information about the app's purpose, target audience, and any specific terminology or jargon used.

3. **Maintain Consistency**: Maintain consistency in the user interface and user experience across all localized versions of your app. This will help users navigate the app seamlessly, regardless of the language they choose.

4. **Consider Text Expansion**: Keep in mind that translated text may expand or contract in length compared to the original text. Design your app's UI to accommodate varying text lengths to prevent layout issues.

5. **Localize App Store Assets**: Localize your app's screenshots, app icons, and promotional materials in the app stores. This will create a cohesive and localized experience for potential users.

6. **Continuous Updates**: As you release updates for your app, ensure that the localized versions are also updated with the latest features and improvements. This will help maintain user engagement and satisfaction.

Implementing app localization in your AppCraft app is a powerful way to expand your user base and provide a personalized experience to users from different regions. By following the steps outlined in this section and adhering to best practices, you can successfully localize your app and make it accessible to a global audience. Embrace app localization as a strategic tool to enhance user engagement and drive the success of your app in the international market.

Thank you for joining us on this journey through AppCraft and app building. In the next section, we will explore troubleshooting and debugging techniques to help you overcome common challenges during the app development process.

Final Thoughts and Thank You

Congratulations on completing "AppCraft: The Ultimate Guide to Building Apps"! You have now gained a solid understanding of the app development process and have learned how to use AppCraft to create your own apps. As you wrap up your journey with this book, it's important to reflect on what you have learned and consider your next steps in the world of app building.

Reflecting on Your AppCraft Experience

Take a moment to reflect on your experience with AppCraft. Think about the challenges you faced, the skills you acquired, and the progress you made throughout the book. Consider the apps you created and the features you implemented. Reflecting on your journey will help you appreciate how far you've come and identify areas for further improvement.

AppCraft is a powerful tool that empowers you to bring your app ideas to life. By mastering the concepts and techniques covered in this book, you have gained the skills necessary to create functional and visually appealing apps. Whether you plan to build apps for personal use, for clients, or for the wider market, AppCraft provides you with a solid foundation to build upon.

Continuing Your App Building Journey

Now that you have completed this book, you may be wondering what your next steps should be. Here are a few suggestions to help you continue your app building journey:

Explore Advanced AppCraft Techniques

While this book covers a wide range of topics, there is always more to learn. Consider exploring advanced AppCraft techniques to further enhance your app building skills. Dive deeper into custom code integration, advanced app features, and app performance optimization. By expanding your knowledge, you can create even more sophisticated and high-performing apps.

Stay Up-to-Date with AppCraft Updates and Trends

The world of app development is constantly evolving, and it's important to stay up-to-date with the latest updates and trends in AppCraft. Follow the official AppCraft website, join relevant forums and communities, and subscribe to newsletters or blogs that provide insights into new features, best practices, and emerging trends. By staying informed, you can leverage the latest tools and techniques to stay ahead of the curve.

Collaborate with Other App Builders

Building apps doesn't have to be a solitary endeavor. Consider joining app development communities or attending local meetups to connect with other app builders. Collaborating with like-minded individuals can provide valuable insights, feedback, and support. By sharing your experiences and learning from others, you can grow as an app builder and expand your network.

Start Building Real-World Apps

Now that you have acquired the necessary skills, it's time to put them into practice by building real-world apps. Identify a problem or a need in your own life or in your target audience's life and start working on a solution. Building real-world apps will not only help you gain practical experience but also provide you with a portfolio to showcase your skills to potential clients or employers.

Thank You!

Writing "AppCraft: The Ultimate Guide to Building Apps" has been a labor of love, and I want to express my sincere gratitude to you for choosing this book as your learning resource. I hope that it has provided you with the knowledge and confidence to embark on your app building journey.

I would also like to extend my thanks to the team at AppCraft for creating such a powerful and user-friendly app building software. Their dedication to providing a seamless and intuitive experience has made it possible for aspiring app builders like yourself to bring their ideas to life.

Remember, app building is a continuous learning process. Embrace the challenges, stay curious, and never stop exploring new possibilities. With determination and perseverance, you have the potential to create innovative and impactful apps that can change lives.

Best of luck on your app building journey, and thank you once again for choosing "AppCraft: The Ultimate Guide to Building Apps"!

This is a link to use free trial or purchase Appcraft.io: https://appcraft.ai?fpr=orvillearrindell30

www.ingramcontent.com/pod-product-compliance
Lightning Source LLC
LaVergne TN
LVHW051737050326
832903LV00023B/968